A Matter of Style

A Matter of Style

A practical guide for GCE candidates at O- and A-level

O. M. Thomson
MA (Cantab.), BA (Lond.)

Hutchinson

London   Melbourne   Sydney   Auckland   Johannesburg

Hutchinson & Co. (Publishers) Ltd

An imprint of the Hutchinson Publishing Group

17-21 Conway Street, London W1P 6JD

Hutchinson Publishing Group (Australia) Pty Ltd
16-22 Church Street, Hawthorn, Melbourne, Victoria 3122

Hutchinson Group (NZ) Ltd
32-34 View Road, PO Box 40-086, Glenfield, Auckland 10

Hutchinson Group (SA) (Pty) Ltd
PO Box 337, Bergvlei 2012, South Africa

First published 1973
Reprinted 1977, 1978
Second edition 1982
Reprinted 1983, 1984

© O. M. Thomson 1973, 1982

Set in Baskerville

Printed and bound in Great Britain by
Anchor Brendon Ltd, Tiptree, Essex

British Library Cataloguing in Publication Data

Thomson, Oscar Mark
  A matter of style. – 2nd ed.
  1. English language – Composition and exercises
  I. Title
  428'.2   PE1112

ISBN 0 09 144541 8

Contents

Foreword

*I just adored this film. . . . Her books have got a lot of power. . . .
The mountains looked really lovely. . . . These programmes are so
boring. . . . This poem has got a marvellous rhythm to it. . . . Romeo
had one bit of awful luck. . . . Lady Macbeth was definitely a
courageous woman. . . . Ophelia loved Hamlet very much, and this
comes over to the reader. . . .*

– every teacher of GCE English will recognize the faults of
style contained in those sentences; for they have a way of
turning up, in strength, in one form or another, every time
a class hands in a batch of essays to be marked. They
appear more frequently than grammatical faults, and they
are more difficult to explain and correct. Yet most English
class-books do not deal with them at all. One can look
through dozens of chapters, in different books, on composition, style, vocabulary, common errors, and so on, and
find no mention of them. In this book I have gathered them
together. I have collected the typical faults of style that
appear, over and over again, in the written work of GCE
students, and I have tried to explain the nature of each one
of them in a not-too-academic, common-sense way.

The two ways of using the book

The students can either work through it, studying the
explanations and examples and doing the exercises that
come at the end of each section. Or they can start with the
exercises at the back. This is quite a good way too, since
these are general exercises, and in order to do them
students will need to refer to all the points of style that are
mentioned in the book.

1 Short sentences

Short sentences demand complete clarity of thought. They cannot be written without it. Long sentences, on the other hand, because they can so easily become shapeless and disorganized, and be badly written, provide an excuse for avoiding it. That is why some students go in for long sentences and avoid short ones. Of course they do not reason it out like that: instead – if they think about it at all – they decide that short sentences sound abrupt, or immature, or too simple, and that long ones sound impressive. No student who clings to that idea will ever improve. For it is not only a mistake: it is also an excuse for avoiding the labour of thinking clearly.

Short sentences are splendid. They do not sound immature. On the contrary, they give an impression of clarity and strength. Sometimes their presence in a piece of writing produces a fine effect of dignified simplicity. Consider, for example, this passage from *The Glory that was Greece*, by J. C. Stobart:

> The Mediterranean is a sheltered sea. Chains of islands, like stepping stones, invite the timid mariner to venture across it. He can sail from Greece to Asia without losing sight of land. On the west it is not so. Greece and Italy turn their backs on one another. Their neighbouring coasts are the harbourless ones.

A student will do well to write plenty of short sentences. His writing will be better because it has them in it, scattered through it, giving it variety and clarifying the thought.

Now here are some passages which you can invigorate by

re-shaping them in such a way that they include some short sentences. First, rewrite this passage so as to divide it into three sentences, of which the last two are short:

> The school Vanessa attended for the next two years was run in a strict but kindly manner by an elderly parson, and she loved it, because the discipline gave her a sense of security.

Now divide this passage into three sentences, using only twelve words:

> He tapped on the window, but there was no answer and so he tapped again.

Divide this into three sentences, using only four words for the third one:

> There is a moment's pause and then, in a quiet voice, Macduff asks Macbeth why he killed the grooms, showing that he is already suspicious.

Divide this passage into four sentences, instead of two, using only three words for the last one:

> Hardy's poetry is quite different from Wordsworth's, being more detailed and closer to nature. Wordsworth, who regarded himself as a philosopher as well as a poet, is often pretentious, but Hardy never is.

2 Long sentences

A *good* long sentence is a unity. Its different parts are so closely related that if a break were made between them it would disturb the flow of thought.

> Suddenly I put my hand upon my mother's arm, for I had heard, in the silent, frosty air, a sound that brought my heart into my mouth – the tap-tapping of the blind man's stick upon the frozen road. (From *Treasure Island*)

Some long sentences are not unities at all: they are long simply because a number of separate statements, which should have had a sentence each, have been bundled together.

> I looked out of the window to see what the weather was like and because it was fine I grabbed hold of my fishing-rod, ran out of the door and started hurrying across the fields towards the river.

Never write a sentence like that one. Whenever you have completed a clear-cut self-contained statement, no matter how short it is, stop. Never put a conjunction at the end of it, instead of a full stop, and run straight through into what should be a new sentence. If you do, you will succeed in writing a sentence that is long simply because it is bad – like the one that has just been quoted. It should have been three sentences:

> I looked out of the window to see what the weather was like. It was fine. So I grabbed hold of my fishing-rod, ran out of the door and started hurrying across the fields towards the river.

Here are some more examples:

The most exciting holiday I ever had was a Mediterranean cruise and it lasted two months.

The most exciting holiday I ever had was a Mediterranean cruise. It lasted two months.

David Copperfield is filled with all sorts of strange characters, and perhaps the most fascinating one of all is Uriah Heep.

David Copperfield is filled with all sorts of strange characters. Perhaps the most fascinating one of all is Uriah Heep.

They had no sympathy for her but criticized the untidiness of the kitchen and complained that the towels were dirty.

They had no sympathy for her. They criticized the untidiness of the kitchen and complained that the towels were dirty.

It is equally bad to join together two separate statements by using a participle (which is a word that ends in *-ing*):

The boy was horrified by the thought of what he had done, being so unnerved by it that he did not dare to go back into the room.

The boy was horrified by the thought of what he had done. He was so unnerved by it that he did not dare to go back into the room.

Hamlet did not place enough value on straightforward, practical deeds, allowing himself instead to lapse into moods of doubt and melancholy.

Hamlet did not place enough value on straight-forward, practical deeds. Instead, he allowed himself to lapse into moods of doubt and melancholy.

These chapters reveal only the surface of her character, its deeper aspects not being revealed until we see her at home with her family.

These chapters reveal only the surface of her character. Its deeper aspects are not revealed until we see her at home with her family.

Here are four long sentences. In some of them – but not all – the writer has run together, into one sentence, what should have been expressed in two. Will you decide which these badly written passages are, and rewrite them in the form of two sentences:

The universe contains millions of stars which are capable of supporting planetary systems, but they lie at vast distances from the earth and it would take some hundreds of light-years to reach them.

One of the great advantages of hang-gliding is that it is a wonderfully silent sport, and as you float over the countryside the only sound is the rush of air past the wings.

Gradually we hauled ourselves up the side of the cliff, digging our toes deep into the crevices and clutching hold of the strongest tufts of grass within reach.

William Golding is one of the most distinguished novelists of recent times, his best known work being *Lord of the Flies*, but he has written a number of other equally original novels.

3 Short and long together

Good writers continually vary the length of their sentences. As a matter of course they avoid writing too many long ones, or too many short ones, one after the other.

Sometimes – to obtain extra force, by making the contrast as sharp as possible – a writer will put a very short sentence after a series of long ones. Here is a passage written by Somerset Maugham. It comes from his essay on Henry Fielding:

> There are some people who cannot read *Tom Jones*. I am not thinking of those who never read anything but the newspapers and the illustrated weeklies, or of those who never read anything but detective stories; I am thinking of those who would not demur if you classed them as members of the intelligentsia, of those who read and re-read *Pride and Prejudice* with delight, *Middlemarch* with self-complacency, and *The Golden Bowl* with reverence. The chances are that it has never occurred to them to read *Tom Jones*; but, sometimes, they have tried and not been able to get on with it. It bores them.

That is splendid writing. There is continual variety. The last sentence in particular, by tightening the rhythm, gives the whole passage an air of alertness and vigour. Here is another example, from the same essay:

> Fielding's enemies accused him of being a political hireling. He was.

Again, by means of a simple contrast between long and short, a little sentence has been loaded with emphasis.

13

The effect will be the opposite if long sentences are written one after the other, without the relief of shorter ones. Then there will be no sense of rhythm, no rise and fall of emphasis. Slackness will prevail, and the reader will find it heavy going.

Will you now rewrite each of the following passages in the form of two sentences, and in such a way that a short sentence is contrasted with a longer one. In most of the passages – but not in all – the short sentence comes second:

All through the following term, for two hours a week, Paul was made to study Latin, which he hated.

It was a grey November morning, and a thin rain was blowing in from the sea, and huge waves were pounding the rocks off Tregenny Point.

For the layman this is probably the best account of the technique of space travel that has yet been written, being both clear and concise.

When he returned home he saw at once, to his great distress, that a change had come over his mother and that she looked older and more frail.

At this point two members of the team became convinced that the guide had taken the wrong path and so they turned back, with the intention of following the old route across the south face, but were never seen again.

4 Questions

A paragraph should deal with one main topic only. Its opening sentence, or sentences, should indicate what the topic is to be. A pleasing effect can sometimes be obtained by putting the opening sentence into the form of a question, to which the rest of the paragraph is the answer.

> The next point that we will consider is whether we put people in prison to reform them or to punish them.

That sentence (the opening one of a paragraph) does its job. But its tone is forbiddingly heavy.

> Do we put people in prison to reform them or to punish them?

In this form it is lighter and clearer. Instead of dragging the style down, it enlivens it.

Questions sound well, too, when introduced during the course of an argument. In a neat, concise way they make its logic plain: *Why? . . . But is this true? . . . How did he do it?*

Here are some heavily worded paragraph-openings. Will you lighten them by re-phrasing them in the form of questions. The number of words to which each one can be reduced is given in brackets:

> I will begin this essay by trying to find the answer to the question of what the purpose of art is.   (6)

> The question of whether or not there are any advantages in being an only child is the next matter that must occupy our attention.   (9)

15

We will now consider what the reason is that this kind of music has suddenly become so popular. (10)

We will now enquire into the cause of Hamlet's hesitation. (4)

Let us now consider the matter of how these changes will affect people's lives. (7)

5 Dead words

Very, quite, extremely, completely, utterly, rather, really, absolutely, definitely – there is nothing wrong with these words, but there is something wrong with throwing in one or other of them with almost every adjective or adverb you use. For some students a statement is never *true*, but always *very true*. For them Chaucer's Summoner is never *a wicked man*, but always *a rather wicked man*, or *a really wicked man*. For them so-and-so is never *astonished*, but always *absolutely astonished*. *Definitely* leaves an odd impression of childish triumph: *Macbeth definitely had a conscience*. ('There! I've made up my mind about *that*.') You should think carefully before using this word, since it nearly always weakens rather than strengthens the meaning.

These qualifying words should be handled with caution. The writer who qualifies nearly every statement he makes, emptily and thoughtlessly, is littering his writing with dead words – words that blunt his meaning instead of sharpening it.

Will you now rewrite these sentences exactly as they stand but leaving out any unnecessary words. The number of words needed is given in brackets. As you finish rewriting each sentence compare your version with the longer one and decide which you think is better:

His courage really was absolutely magnificent.   (4)

It was definitely a somewhat frightening experience. (5)

The overcoming of a disability very often strengthens a person's character quite considerably. (10)

This is definitely one of Hardy's very best poems. (7)

Gliding really is a most fascinating sport. (5)

These changes, which were forced through by a group of very incompetent bureaucrats, have completely and utterly destroyed the village. (16)

6 Dead expressions

It is interesting to note that. . . . – this remark kills all interest. *It is safe to say that. . . .* – perhaps the writer could have taken a risk, and just said it? *It would not be an exaggeration to say that. . . . It is worthy of note that. . . . There is no doubt that. . . . There is reason to believe that* (but the reason is never revealed) *. . . .It is worth pointing out that. . . .* – laboured remarks of this kind are often nothing more than padding.

In some respects. . . . From certain points of view. . . . In some ways. . . . In a way. . . . Somehow. . . . On the whole. . . . – all these expressions are empty of meaning unless the writer goes on to explain *what* respects he has in mind, or *what* points of view, or *what* ways, or why he has qualified his statement by putting *on the whole* in front of it.

Tends to. . . . Has a tendency to. . . . Helps to. . . . Seems to. . . . Serves to. . . . are often used emptily.

This speech tends to deepen our sympathy for him. (This speech deepens. . . .)

This conversation helps to emphasize the difference between Brutus and Cassius. (This conversation emphasizes. . . .)

This incident seems to heighten the tension. (This incident heightens. . . .)

This speech serves to emphasize Duncan's kindness. (This speech emphasizes. . . .)

So, too, are *succeeds in* and *manages to*.

The poet succeeds in creating a colourful picture. (The poet creates. . . .)

Chaucer manages to convey a clear impression of the Monk's hypocrisy. (Chaucer conveys. . . .)

Expressions like that last one have a faintly patronizing tone ('Well done, Chaucer').

Now rewrite these sentences, leaving out the unnecessary words:

I must state in the most forthright terms that I definitely disagree with this view.   (2)

The characters in this book certainly do tend to come vividly to life.   (9)

It must be said that Orwell's satire really is absolutely deadly.   (4)

It would not be an exaggeration to say that it was a rather lonely job.   (5)

It is safe to say that the most important requirement of a novel is that it should have a really good story to it.   (15)

I will begin by pointing out that there is absolutely no truth whatever in this statement.   (7)

7 'Also'

Also often sounds ugly when placed at the beginning of a sentence:

> Also he could play the trumpet.

Taken into the flow of the sentence, it sounds much better:

> He could also play the trumpet.

> Also this speech reveals a certain weakness in Juliet's character.

> This speech also reveals a certain weakness in Juliet's character.

> Also he was the strongest boy in the group.

> He was also the strongest boy in the group.

In these sentences *also* is used lightly, without emphasis, in the sense of 'in addition', or 'as well'. Sometimes more stress is laid on it. Standing awkwardly at the head of a sentence, often with a comma after it, it is made to do duty as *moreover* – that is to say, it is used to show that a new line of thought, or a new idea, is being introduced:

> Also, they never expected that this threat would be taken seriously.

> Also, as soon as we began to consider this route we found that certain parts of it had never been properly mapped out.

> Also, however hard they tried to disguise the fact, many of the poets of that generation were more interested in politics than art.

In contexts like these it is nearly always better to use *moreover*. Try re-reading those three sentences with *moreover* as the first word, and you will notice the improvement.

Now improve each of the following sentences by moving the *also* forward:

Also this film has been shown in France and America.

Also she gave him her father's gold watch.

Also mountaineering can be a very humbling experience.

Also Surrey is a very beautiful county.

Also these rare birds can be seen occasionally in the north of Scotland.

8 Incomplete sentences

Occasionally, in order to achieve some particular effect, a writer may leave a sentence, or a series of sentences, incomplete:

> A grey, wet day. A high wind ruffling the poplars. Rain flowing like a waterfall over the pavilion roof.

There, the aim is to suggest that the writer is making a swift sketch of the scene, in a few brisk strokes.

> Been alarmed, have you, by this latest trend? Not to worry. Not unduly, anyway. Because here are the facts. . . .

The writer of that newspaper item wants us to feel that we are listening to a matey sort of bloke who is just chatting to us in his natural manner.

There is no harm in writing incomplete sentences if you have some special reason for doing so. But it is quite a different matter if you leave them incomplete not deliberately, in order to gain an effect, but through carelessness:

> Today the world seems a very small place. A good bit smaller, in fact, than a single country would have seemed fifty years ago. Business men travelling to distant capitals as a matter of routine. Television linking together people who live thousands of miles apart. Quite different from earlier times.

That writer simply followed the disjointed patterns of casual, everyday chat; and he did so because that was what came most easily to him. He had no particular purpose in mind. Incomplete sentences of that kind spoil written English. They make it seem slapdash and poorly conceived.

Will you now rewrite that last passage (about the world seeming small) in such a way that all the sentences are complete. Re-shape it and re-word it in any way you like, but do not alter the meaning.

9 Tenses

Never switch about from one tense to another. To do so is sheer carelessness. Here are some examples of this very irritating mistake:

> It was a cold December night. It is snowing hard, but the sitting-room, where we are having our coffee, was warm and comfortable.

> Outside, it was much darker than we expected it to be, because the wind has swept a bank of cloud across the sky, obscuring the moon and the stars.

> We moved forward at a steady pace. On either side of us the trees rustled, making us wonder if ghosts are lurking there.

> The Wife of Bath is heavily over-dressed. She wore a huge hat, bright red stockings, and new shoes.

> Iago persuades Roderigo to go to Cyprus even before he has decided exactly what use he was going to make of him.

Will you now rewrite those passages in such a way as to eliminate the inconsistencies in the use of tenses. In the three narrative passages it will be best to keep to the past tense. But in the three about literature the present tense will probably be more suitable. When writing answers to literature questions you will often find it convenient to use the present. Chaucer is dead; but he is not dead as a writer – so we can write: 'Chaucer brings this character vividly to life.' Hamlet lived long ago; but fictitious characters do not die – so we can write: 'Hamlet is tormented by doubts.'

10 'So' and 'such'

Never use *so* or *such* purely to emphasize a straightforward statement.

> The meeting was so interesting.

> He was so disappointed.

> She laughed in such a sweet way.

> It was such a surprise to him.

> The music was so beautiful.

All those sentences sound silly and sentimental because *so* and *such* have been wrongly used. Whenever one or other of these words is used in this sort of context the sentence must be continued into a second clause introduced by the word *that*. In those sentences, therefore, we must either leave out the *so*'s and the *such*'s or else we must write:

> The meeting was so interesting that I was sorry when it came to an end.

> He was so disappointed that he leant on my shoulder and wept.

> She laughed in such a sweet way that everyone turned to look at her.

> It was such a surprise to him that he nearly fainted.

> The music was so beautiful that it made me catch my breath.

Notice, however, that sometimes, when they occur in subordinate clauses, *so* and *such* can be used as emphasizing words without producing a bad effect:

All the delegates were young. That is why the meeting was such a triumphant success.

A person who is so careless, over such a simple matter, cannot be trusted.

In three of the following sentences the *so* or the *such* should not be there. Will you write those three sentences out, leaving out the unwanted words:

The ending of the play was so sad that I could hardly bear to watch it.

She liked living there because it was such a lonely place.

He had such a wonderful gift for understanding people.

The weather was so perfect.

We had not realized that he could be so obstinate.

A holiday by the sea is so much more exciting when there are opportunities for surfing and yachting.

11 'Is when'

In most contexts *is when* does not make sense.

> A good view of the lake is when you reach the top of the path.

We cannot write 'when you reach' unless something happens in the first part of the sentence, and in that case nothing does. So we will *make* something happen, and then the *when* will have something to attach itself to:

> You *get* a good view of the lake when you reach the top of the path.

Here is another example:

> The climax of the film is when Joe is murdered.

This time it will be more convenient to leave the first part of the sentence unaltered, and have nothing happen, and get rid of the *when*:

> The climax of the film is the murder of Joe.

Here are some more examples:

> The Council's worst mistake was when they allowed these flats to be built.

> The Council made their worst mistake when they allowed these flats to be built.

Or:

> The Council's worst mistake was to allow these flats to be built.

A good example of Chaucer's sly humour is when he describes the Nun's table manners.

Chaucer's description of the Nun's table manners is a good example of his sly humour.

The most dramatic scene is in the churchyard when the convict confronts Pip.

The most dramatic scene is the one in which the convict confronts Pip in the churchyard.

A further simile is when Tennyson likens the mountain stream to a 'downward smoke'.

In a further simile Tennyson likens the mountain stream to a 'downward smoke'.

Such expressions as *the scene where, the scene when, the chapter where*, are also unpleasantly inaccurate.

The scene where Duncan and Banquo arrive. . . .

The scene in which Duncan and Banquo arrive. . . .

The chapter where Wells describes Mr Polly's education. . . .

The chapter in which Wells describes Mr Polly's education. . . .

Now re-shape these sentences:

The most unexpected event in the film is when the hidden documents are discovered.

One of the worst disasters of that decade was when the *Titanic* sank.

A big surprise was when we turned the corner and saw that the road was blocked.

The deepest kind of silence is when it comes suddenly and unexpectedly.

A simile is when you liken one thing to another.

Caesar's last words are when he says 'Et tu, Brute?'

Brutus's great blunder was when he decided to allow Antony to address the citizens.

12 'This', 'which' and 'showing'

His most recent novel was hailed by one critic as a minor classic. This pleased him enormously.

When we read that sentence we understand at once what the *this* refers back to. But people sometimes use a *this* at the beginning of a sentence when what it refers back to is not clear at all:

As we approached the house we could see at a glance that certain parts of it were badly in need of repair – especially the beautiful mansard roof which the agent had praised so highly. This was a great disappointment to us.

For a moment the reader is misled into thinking that it was the roof which was the disappointment – which of course it was; but that is not what the writer meant.

Which is sometimes used in the same misleading way:

If you take this road into Oxford you get many glimpses, from far off, of its beautiful clusters of spires and of Magdalen's sturdy tower, which makes you eager to reach the city and explore it.

Is it Magdalen's tower that makes you eager? Is that what the writer meant?

Finally, the word *showing* is sometimes used loosely too – that is, in such a way that it is not clearly related to what the writer intended it to refer to:

The protest against the threatened closure of the

theatre was so widely supported that the Council finally agreed to allow it to remain open, showing how popular this repertory company has become in our town.

It is true that the Council's change of heart did show, indirectly, how popular the company had become, but that is not what the writer meant.

Will you now look back to the first muddled piece of writing we considered – about the house in need of repair – and rewrite the second sentence in such a way as to get rid of the misleading *this*.

Next, look at the second passage, about Oxford. Assume that you are writing it and that you have got as far as putting the comma after 'tower'. Now complete the rest of it in such a way as to get rid of the muddle caused by the *which*.

Now rewrite the last part of the last passage, about the closure of the theatre. Again, assume that you are writing it and that you have got as far as 'open', but instead of a comma you have put a full stop there. Now complete it. How are you going to begin that last sentence? Ask yourself, 'Exactly what was it that showed how popular the repertory company had become?'

13 Pronouns

Pronouns give a splendid effect of clarity and economy. You should use them whenever you can. Use them even when there may seem to be a risk of confusion. For they have a much stronger tendency to attach themselves to the right nouns than many people realize. A reader is not going to insist, perversely, on attaching them to the wrong ones, against the sense of a passage, just in order to make nonsense of it.

Here, now, are seven passages. Will you rewrite the second sentence of each one in such a way that you do not repeat *any* of the nouns mentioned in the first sentence, but use pronouns instead. As you complete the rewriting of each one, read over what you have written and notice how much more fluent the English sounds when the pronouns are used:

John was terrified of Mr Bates. Yet John bravely confronted Mr Bates and ordered Mr Bates to leave.

My favourite painter is David Hockney. David Hockney's best pictures, in my opinion, are fine works of art.

Anne's attempts to persuade her father that the programme was harmless were of no avail. Anne's father would not let Anne watch the programme.

Carol decided that a pearl brooch would set off her black dress perfectly. So Carol went out that afternoon and bought a pearl brooch.

There have been many explanations of the origin of human life. The oldest explanation is that God created human life.

Chaucer describes the Pardoner in a tone of sneering contempt. We are left in no doubt that Chaucer despises the Pardoner.

Soon after leaving Juliet, Romeo approaches Friar Laurence. Romeo tells Friar Laurence of his love for Juliet and asks for Friar Laurence's help.

14 Doubling conjunctions

A word like *which* can be used twice in the same sentence in order to introduce two parallel clauses:

These documents, which he carried in a brief-case, and which he claimed were genuine, were in fact a bundle of forgeries.

There is nothing wrong in using *which* twice in that way. But if we use it twice in such a way as to make the second clause it introduces dependent on the first one, we shall produce a clumsy sentence:

These documents, which he carried in a brief-case, which he kept locked, were in fact. . . .

What is true of *which* is true of other conjunctions too. The following sentences are all clumsy because in each one the conjunction is doubled:

We were disappointed when we revisited this part of the coast because it had been completely spoilt because a big caravan site had been put there.

When you visit poor countries you begin to think how fortunate you are when you see children begging for food.

Some people think that space travel is a waste of money. But this great adventure cannot be measured in terms of money alone, but perhaps too much is spent on it.

Will you now improve those three passages. Re-shape them as much as you like, but do not alter the meaning.

15 Prepositions

Prepositions are sometimes used in a way which is unpleasantly inaccurate, as in the following examples. The correction is given in brackets.

This scene makes a sharp contrast from the previous one (with).

The underlying theme in his speech . . . (of).

The poem has a regular rhythm to it. (The poem has a regular rhythm.)

There was a lack of understanding by the men (on the part of).

They gathered by the untidiness of the kitchen that she had left in a hurry (from).

With the Summoner Chaucer's attitude is quite different. (Chaucer's attitude towards the Summoner is quite different.)

Chaucer adopts a different method with the Friar (when describing).

The scenes with Laertes . . . (in which Laertes appears).

Lear expresses his feelings with words that summon up vague suggestions of time and vastness (in).

Iago replied, with a tone of bitter contempt, that he would never speak another word (in).

Now improve these sentences:

She had a wide knowledge on these matters.

By what we heard we could only conclude that he had left home.

We were unable to obtain any information on this.

They had left no clue of where they had gone.

Juliet expresses her grief with words that are deeply poetical.

The scene with Banquo murdered is one of the best in the play.

16 Tautology

Tautology is the useless repetition of the same idea in different words. Two words of similar meaning are used when one would have done:

The heartbreak and the despair.

Compassion and pity.

She hated and resented him.

Shrewd and perceptive.

Troubled and anxious.

A wicked villain.

A sudden shock.

A perfect ideal.

Sometimes two phrases, or two sentences, are used:

The tale never becomes monotonous: it is always varied and interesting.

She had a dependable husband – someone she could rely on.

The author keeps to the point and does not wander off into irrelevancies.

He was the prop of her world: without him her world would have collapsed.

The doubt may occasionally arise: is this or that expression a piece of tautology or is it a proper use of two distinct words? A simple test is to ask: could we put *both . . . and also* in front of the words? What about *conflict and strife*? *Both conflict and also strife* is obviously repetitive. What about *sad and tragic*? Could we write *both sad and also tragic*? Perhaps there is a distinction. But, if there is, it is a subtle one, and we are under an obligation to the reader to explain it to him. If we pass it by without referring to it he will rightly conclude that the words are a piece of useless repetition.

Some students have a way of refusing to own up to tautology. Of course no two words have exactly the same meaning, and a writer can easily convince himself afterwards that he used two words instead of one because he was anxious to convey some subtle shade of difference – when in fact he never gave the matter a thought.

Tautology can also take the form of simple repetition: exactly the same point is made twice. The duplication is irritating to the reader:

Throughout the whole chapter. . . .

But after a while, however, he began to realize. . . .

That is how it first began.

At about two o'clock or thereabouts.

Then after that. . . .

The final incident with which the chapter ends. . . .

The experiences they shared together. . . .

These factors combined together to produce. . . .

Apparently he seemed to be unaware. . . .

He will have to try yet harder still.

This was also part of his purpose too.

He could do no more than just follow blindly.

The daily papers that regularly appear. . . .

Now look at these sentences. Six of them contain some form of duplication. Will you rewrite those six in such a way as to eliminate it:

He made the same journey every Tuesday, at exactly the same time.

Inevitably, under these circumstances, he was bound to fail.

At half past six exactly the first batch of evening papers appeared on the streets.

It was nothing more than just a passing phase.

He left home exactly one year ago to the day.

With every year that passed he became more and more embittered.

He showed that he was equally as capable of a sustained effort as any other member of the team.

This alteration made the play even better still.

After a while the moon reappeared again.

17 Forced imagery

Metaphors and similes offer such an obvious way of improving one's writing that a student will sometimes be tempted to introduce one or other of them, not because he needs it to enrich or clarify his meaning, but because he thinks it sounds impressive.

> Chaucer brings the sharp razor edge of his wit to bear on this pilgrim.

> It is through this weak link in Othello's steel personality that Iago stabs.

> The powerful strokes with which he paints his word-pictures. . . .

Those metaphors were conceived and elaborated as examples of 'good writing'. For this reason they sound amateurish and insincere.

> Wells's characters spring up from the page like the cardboard cut-outs in a child's story-book.

That is another self-conscious attempt at a display of literary skill. The simile is not needed. The writer simply meant:

> Wells's characters are cardboard figures.

Learning how to use imagery effectively is not easy. Here is one piece of advice: always use it sincerely – that is to say, introduce a metaphor or a simile only if you think it will clarify or enhance what you are trying to convey, and never because you think it will sound impressive as a piece of writing.

18 Choosing the specific adjective or adverb

Good, bad, badly, brilliant, marvellous, dreadfully, terribly – generalized adjectives and adverbs of this kind are sometimes useful. But more often than not you will find that you can improve your style by being more specific. Try to find the word that will tell the reader not merely that something is *good*, but in what way it is good.

> This is a good portrait . . . a clear portrait? . . . a realistic portrait? . . . a convincing portrait? . . . a life-like portrait? . . . a detailed portrait? . . . an amusing portrait?

> This is a good metaphor . . . an inspired metaphor? . . . a colourful metaphor? . . . a concise metaphor? . . . an original metaphor?

> This is a bad metaphor . . . an unconvincing metaphor? . . . a colourless metaphor? . . . an awkward metaphor? . . . a far-fetched metaphor? . . . a trite metaphor?

> She was a terrible hypocrite . . . a confirmed hypocrite? . . . a shameless hypocrite? . . . a plausible hypocrite?

If you are making a general statement you may find that you can still do better than choose words like *good* or *bad*:

> This is a good simile because. . . . This is an effective simile because. . . .

> What makes this description so good . . . so vivid. . . .

What makes this description so bad . . . so flat. . . .

It may be helpful, sometimes, when choosing an adjective or an adverb, to think of a scale. One end of it is the general end, the other the specific end. Always try to move as far as you can towards the specific end. Often you will find that you can move a long way: *very satisfying*, for example, can be changed to *deeply satisfying; very experienced* to *widely experienced; very overloaded* to *heavily overloaded; brilliant insight* to *sharp insight*, or *shrewd insight; a great dislike* to *a strong dislike*, or *a bitter dislike* – and so on.

Some generalized adverbial expressions, in certain contexts, sound embarrassingly naive:

> Hamlet loved Ophelia very much. (Hamlet loved Ophelia deeply.)

Now suggest a more precise adjective or adverb for each of the following expressions or sentences. Choose a different one each time:

> A good musician. . . . He had a good brain. . . . It was not a very good explanation.

> A bad argument. . . . A bad decision. . . . The discipline was very bad. . . . A bad mistake.

> A marvellous actor. . . . An awful speech. . . . These horrible hoardings ruin the view. . . . A big risk. . . . A big handicap.

> The streets were terribly hot. . . . The sun was terribly bright. . . . He was terrifically intelligent. . . . We were terrifically impressed by his bravery.

19 Choosing the simple word

Some students, as soon as they take up a pen, seem to find it difficult to think of the ordinary, clear words of the language. Instead of *try* they write *endeavour*; instead of *show, demonstrate*; instead of *tell, inform*; instead of *too, excessively*; instead of *long, lengthy*; instead of *begin, commence*; instead of *most of the time, the majority of the time*; instead of *buy, purchase*; instead of *enough, sufficient*; instead of *because, on account of the fact that*; instead of *many, numerous*; instead of *often, on numerous occasions* . . . and so on. They write in this way because they feel that in order to write well they must adopt a learned tone, and choose words that sound impressive. In fact, that is the way to write badly. For a writer's aim should be to convey his meaning as clearly as he can. If, instead, he aims at creating an impression, he will make his meaning less clear, and at the same time sound pompous and foolish.

So never choose the word that is more complicated, or more literary, or more learned, just because you think it sounds impressive. The words that sound truly impressive are the simple ones.

Will you now suggest a simpler word that could replace the more elaborate one that has been used in each of these sentences:

> He exhibited a great deal of courage. . . . We did not anticipate that they would arrive so soon. . . . The village we reside in. . . . They did not need our

assistance. . . . She committed one serious mistake. . . . They are going to construct six houses on this site. . . . The envelope was concealed under a cushion. . . . For the greater proportion of the time. . . . There were approximately forty people in the room. . . . He concluded his speech with an appeal for money.

20 Avoiding the undignified word

A simple style has dignity. A casual style, made up of conversational mannerisms and expressions, has none. In literature answers, especially, slang expressions are liable to cause a collapse into absurdity:

It is difficult to understand what makes Caliban tick.

Then King Lear simply blew up.

In the meanwhile Othello had worked himself up into a really dreadful state.

Even the Queen did not realize that Hamlet was kidding.

Expressions like these are glaringly wrong; but there are many others that are bad in a less obvious way:

The poet puts over the sadness of the scene. (conveys)

Ophelia was scared. (frightened)

Maybe Caliban was right. (Perhaps)

In this scene Macbeth shows quite a bit of feeling. (some feeling)

The pathos of the scene comes over to the reader. (is felt by the reader)

There are quite a few sad moments in this story. (some sad moments)

The poet then brings in a simile. (introduces)

This detail adds a bit of realism to the scene. (a touch of realism)

Keats next talks about the different pictures on the urn. (describes)

In this verse there is a cunning suggestion that . . . (subtle)

A strange sadness hangs around this story. (haunts)

In this scene Macbeth's conscience is bothering him. (troubling)

Then Antony brings up the subject of Caesar's will. (introduces)

Then Cassius brings up another argument. (puts forward)

In this scene another side of Hamlet's character comes out. (is revealed)

Iago found it easy to fool Othello about the handkerchief. (deceive)

After a bit. . . . (After a while. . . . After a few moments. . . .)

Pretty well all the time. . . . (Nearly all the time. . . .)

She had lots more courage than her husband. (far more)

A whole lot of these ideas. . . . (Many of)

This joke always causes lots of laughter. (a great deal of laughter)

We hear an awful lot of bad music today. (a great deal of bad music)

One might just as well make out that it is wrong to keep cows for their milk. (argue . . . maintain)

As soon as his wife has left, Macbeth begins talking to himself. (begins a soliloquy . . . begins to soliloquize)

The world is in an awful mess. (in a troubled state . . . in a chaotic state . . . in a state of conflict and confusion)

Antony then puts on an act of being overcome with grief. (pretends to be)

As far as beauty of form is concerned, the ode 'To Autumn' beats all the other odes. (surpasses)

In this scene an argument starts up between Cassius and Brutus. (begins . . . develops)

Iago keeps on about the handkerchief. (keeps mentioning)

The poet then switches back to his opening theme. (returns)

The poet makes up a vivid picture. (creates)

They were afraid that his speech would start something up. (cause trouble)

Then Hamlet comes on. (appears . . . enters)

After Hamlet has gone off. . . . (left)

Hamlet's next move. . . . (step)

The poet harps on the idea that life is futile. (dwells)

He had one final go at regaining his self-composure. (He made one final attempt to regain his self-composure.)

Here are some more sentences that lack dignity. Will you rewrite them and improve the style:

This unfortunate incident mucked up our holiday.

Some of the more violent scenes on the television turn me up.

One remark he made really stuck in my mind.

Many years ago, before cars had been thought up....

What got me most about this film was the wonderful photography of the mountain scenery.

Claudius thought he could kid Hamlet.

Antony wound up his speech with a moving appeal to the citizens' sense of pity.

21 'Thing'

Thing is a word that often sounds slovenly. Try to replace it with the name of whatever 'thing' it is:

The most dramatic thing in the play. . . . (event . . . incident)

One thing about this writer's style. . . . (One feature of this writer's style. . . .)

All kinds of interesting things are shown on the television. (programmes)

One thing that occurred during the journey upset her deeply. (incident)

The most tragic thing about Ophelia's death. . . . (The most tragic aspect of Ophelia's death. . . .)

In this scene another thing in Hamlet's character is revealed. (another aspect of Hamlet's character. . . . another side of Hamlet's character. . . .)

Iago knows that Othello will imagine all kinds of things. (possibilities)

Stephen's soul was deeply wounded by this kind of thing. (treatment)

Many old people find it difficult to keep in touch with things. (life)

The things he said about his cousin. . . . (The remarks he made)

These things suggest that the Nun paid too much attention to her appearance. (These details)

Things like this give the play a deep sadness. (Touches like this)

This metaphor suggests two things. (two ideas)

The thing that was uppermost in his mind. . . . (The thought)

Will you now rewrite these sentences. In each one, replace *thing* with a more precise word:

To be caught up in this kind of violence is a very frightening thing.

Some of the things he put forward in his speech. . . .

The loss of the R101, in 1930, was one of the worst things in the history of aviation.

The most popular thing in the programme. . . .

In my opinion the preservation of wild life is a thing that is well worth striving for.

The conquest of Mount Everest was a truly heroic thing.

22 'Just' and 'simply'

There is a colloquial use of *just*, before adjectives and verbs, which should always be avoided in writing:

> The audience just loved his singing.

> He was just determined to marry her.

> When he first appears on the stage Edmund is just full of resentment.

> The delay seemed just endless.

In those sentences *just* has been used, not in one of its proper senses, but as a means of emphasizing the word that follows it. If ever you find that you have used it in this way you should cross it out.

Simply, too, is sometimes used in the same way:

> The damage was simply enormous.

> His generosity was simply wonderful.

> Everyone who knew her simply adored her.

In each of those sentences it should be crossed out, since it has been used not in its proper sense, but as a means of emphasis, in a way that is colloquial and childish.

Here are some more sentences in which *just* and *simply* are used. In three of them they are used in a weak sense. Will you write out those three, leaving out the *just* or the *simply*:

> They were only just in time.

> The front of the building was simply proportioned.

He was just over six foot tall.

The view was simply magnificent.

The film lasted just one hour and six minutes.

She just wanted to be left in peace.

She just longed to get married and have children of her own.

He just never arrived on time.

23 'Says', 'calls' and 'gets'

Says, in some contexts, is too colloquial:

> Chaucer says that the Squire is about twenty years of age.

We could write *Chaucer states* instead, or *Chaucer writes*, but both these expressions sound stilted; so we will write:

> Chaucer tells us that the Squire is about twenty years of age.

Here are some more examples:

> As he enters the courtyard Banquo says that the stars are completely hidden (remarks).

> Antony then says that he has no intention of contradicting Brutus (declares).

> Cassius, who was more cautious, said that it would be wiser to delay the attack (argued, maintained).

> Ophelia is heartbroken, and at the end of her speech she says 'O woe is me!' (cries out).

Calls, too, sometimes sounds wrong:

> Chaucer calls the Squire a 'lover and a lusty bachelor'.

> Chaucer describes the Squire as a 'lover and a lusty bachelor'.

> John of Gaunt calls England a 'precious stone set in the silver sea'.

John of Gaunt compares England to a 'precious stone set in the silver sea'.

Gets and *got* are sometimes undignified:

As soon as Banquo gets to the palace gates. . . . (reaches).

This poem has got several metaphors (has).

He got a good reputation in the wars against the heathens (won).

The poet gets this effect by including several unusual adjectives (achieves).

Will you now improve these sentences:

This book has recently got very popular.

After a short delay the train got moving again.

We got to our destination sooner than we expected.

The scenery in this part of the county has got more variety to it.

Only a few moments before he is stabbed Caesar says he is unassailable.

Romeo calls the window at which Juliet appears 'the east' and he says that Juliet herself is 'the sun'.

24 'Add to', 'increase' and 'lessen'

Students sometimes use these verbs loosely, without troubling to find a more exact verb:

This line adds to the poetic effect (heightens).

This scene adds to the tension (heightens).

These details add to the picture (enhance, enrich).

This speech increases the atmosphere of wildness and terror (intensifies).

This aspect of Brutus's character increases the contrast between him and Cassius (sharpens).

This digression lessens the monotony (relieves).

There was not a trace of sunlight to lessen the gloom (relieve, lighten).

This line lessens the effect of the poem as a whole (weakens).

It is not suggested that 'add to', 'increase' or 'lessen' are necessarily wrong, or even bad, in all the above examples – merely that the style is improved, in each case, if the word given in brackets is used instead.

Will you now improve the following sentences in the same way:

These touches add to the sadness of the play.

These details increase the realism of the scene.

This knowledge increased our awareness of the dangers we were facing.

As the hours went by the gloom increased.

The inclusion of a harp in the orchestra greatly adds to this piece of music.

This disappointment lessened his enthusiasm.

The slight pause he made added to the impact of his reply.

25 Abstract expressions

Always express your ideas in as direct a manner as possible. Some people have a way of introducing abstract nouns into their writing quite unnecessarily, with the result that what could have been a perfectly straightforward statement becomes obscure:

> The occurrence of the mistake was due to our inability to read his writing.

In other words:

> The mistake occurred because we could not read his writing.

> The reason for her despising her husband was that he was lazy.

> She despised her husband because he was lazy.

> The other children picked on her because of her smallness and timidity.

> The other children picked on her because she was small and timid.

> This setback brought about a strengthening of his determination.

> This setback strengthened his determination.

> There is a great deal of irregularity in the metre.

> The metre is very irregular.

> There is a complete absence of imagery in this poem.

There is no imagery in this poem.

Caesar had an acute awareness of this flaw in his character.

Caesar was acutely aware of this flaw in his character.

Chaucer has admiration for the Knight.

Chaucer admires the Knight.

There is also a mention by Chaucer of the Monk's love of hunting.

Chaucer also mentions the Monk's love of hunting.

Now re-shape these sentences in such a way that the meaning is expressed in a direct manner:

He was dismissed because of his refusal to obey the rules.

The beauty of the view was so great that we did not want to leave.

It will take three more days to achieve the completion of the task.

These changes will bring about a great improvement in the play.

The steepness of the slope was such that we were able to move forward only very slowly.

26 Active and passive

The active form of the verb is clear and direct. You should never twist it into the passive when there is no need to.

> In earlier times a much more important part was played in people's lives by religion.

> In earlier times religion played a much more important part in people's lives.

> The main block is led up to by a long drive, lined with trees.

> A long drive, lined with trees, leads up to the main block.

> In this chapter a very clear idea is conveyed by William Golding of the meaning behind the story.

> In this chapter William Golding conveys a very clear idea of the meaning behind the story.

> Roderigo's infatuation with Desdemona is made use of by Iago.

> Iago makes use of Roderigo's infatuation with Desdemona.

In all those examples the passive form is bad because it is not really a passive at all, but an active form clumsily twisted round. There is nothing wrong with a true passive:

> They found him lying near a ditch: he had been knocked down and robbed.

The passive forms which occur in the following sentences

are all clumsy and unnecessary. Will you rewrite the sentences and change these forms into the active:

In his speech this point was very clearly explained by him.

A firm of architects have now bought the house, and an undertaking has been given by them not to alter it in any way.

A touch of humour is added to the film by the sudden appearance of this eccentric character.

This scene is brought vividly to life by Lawrence.

The longings of a downtrodden people are expressed by this song.

The witches are first encountered by Macbeth when he is making his way across the heath with Banquo.

27 Full stops and commas

Two mistakes are always being made. They are made so often that they could be described as the two curses of students' writing. One is putting a comma, instead of a full stop, at the end of a sentence that is grammatically complete:

> Cambridge is a beautiful city, its most impressive features are its wide quadrangles and the quiet meadows that form a background to them.

A comma should never be used, as it has been in that passage, to separate one sentence from another. In that case, as it happens, the reader is not muddled by the mistake. But that was pure luck – because he very often will be:

> It is unlikely that this stretch of meadowland will ever be spoilt, because it contains such a wonderful variety of wild life, and also perhaps because they respect its beauty, the College Governors have made an order that it must never be built on.

The other mistake is using only one comma when two are needed. Two commas are often used to enclose a group of words and set them aside from the rest of the sentence. They work in partnership, as a pair:

> There is a tradition, dating back to medieval times, that the waters of this lake have healing properties.

In that sentence we pause for both the commas; so neither of them is likely to get missed out. But very often we do not pause at all for the first one of the pair:

It would be easy, I think, to lose your way on these moors.

This, then, is the conclusion I have reached.

By the end of the week, however, the situation had changed.

In sentences like those we must be especially careful to put in the first of the two commas, because the voice passes over it so quickly that it is easy to forget it.

In the following passage the ends of some of the sentences have been marked by commas instead of full stops. Will you write it out and put these mistakes right:

These two old people lived on their own, and often they felt lonely. For many years their son, who was their only child, had lived with them, now he had grown up and left home, and they hardly ever saw him. Their house was very isolated, their nearest neighbours lived nearly a mile away, and so their only companions were the birds and animals in the woods. But on this particular evening they did not feel lonely, they had a guest, their nephew, Derek, whom they had known since he had been a child, was staying with them.

In the next passage four commas are missing. Will you write it out, with those commas put in:

Derek had arrived early that afternoon. He had taken a taxi which was the only form of transport, from Littledean Station. The roads were almost snowbound. A blizzard had raged the taxi driver told him, all the previous day. No gritting it seemed, was ever undertaken in those remote country districts, for the surfaces of all the roads particularly at the sides, were corrugated into white trenches.

63

28 Colons, semi-colons and dashes

A colon marks the end of a sentence, just as a full stop does. But it differs from a full stop in this respect: it tells the reader that in the next sentence there is going to be an explanation of what has just been said. When we are reading aloud and we come to a colon we do not lower the voice fully, as we do for a full stop: we keep it half raised and expectant.

This route had two serious disadvantages: it was very steep, and in some places the path had crumbled away.

They soon found out what had caused the derailment: a section of the line had fractured.

He will not be able to compete tomorrow: he has torn a ligament in his ankle.

This plan has one great weakness: it makes no allowance for even the smallest error of judgement.

A semi-colon has none of the forward-pointing momentum that a colon has. It is like a weak full stop: it ends a sentence, as a full stop does, but more gently. You should use one when you feel that a full stop would mark your sentence off too sharply from the one that follows:

It is a dull time of year. The amusement parks are closed for the winter; the promenade is deserted.

Time works its changes. Great men become famous and then die and are forgotten; empires rise and fall;

wars are fought, and there is suffering and destruction.

Semi-colons should be used sparingly. A write who throws them in freely, when they are not really needed, all through his work, instead of ending his sentences properly with full stops, makes his writing look casual and slapdash.

A dash is a useful punctuation mark. It can be used to direct the reader's attention forward to a single word, or to a short phrase:

She accused him of giving way to the weakness he despised most – cowardice.

His character is like his clothes – dull and shabby.

He had one fatal weakness – a love of flattery.

Commas in these sentences, instead of dashes, would not be right.

A writer may also use a dash if he wants to add an afterthought to something he has just written, or if he wants to make a brief comment on it:

He was very pleased with the decision they reached at last week's committee meeting – or at least he said he was.

They decided to take the path that led across the mountains by the northern pass – a dangerous route.

Tempted in this way, Cassio gets drunk – not helplessly, but enough for Iago's purposes.

Dashes can also be used in pairs to mark off a parenthesis. They mark it off more sharply than commas do, and they should be used when commas would not be sharp enough:

On the contrary – and this is the important point – it

was only because he did not know what he was doing that he succeeded so brilliantly.

If we turn to Hazlitt – and there is no greater critic – we will find a different opinion expressed.

Othello's finest qualities – his courage, his honesty, the aristocratic pride that he never loses – are all revealed.

Finally, a dash can be used to pull a sentence together, usually after a list:

Manly courage, honesty, and kindness of heart – these were the qualities that made Prince Henry so popular among all classes of Englishmen.

Six of the commas are wrong in the next passage: two of them should have been colons, and four of them dashes. Write the passage out with these mistakes put right:

Derek was a town-bred boy, and in his view country life had one great drawback, there was nothing to do in the evenings. The time between supper and bedtime always passed very slowly, so slowly, in fact, that Derek sometimes found himself wishing that he had never come on the visit. On this particular evening, after reading a magazine for a while, he did what he had done on every previous evening that week, he made his excuses to his uncle and aunt and went to bed early.

His bedroom, it was really his uncle's study converted into a bedroom, was on the ground floor, and its window faced directly on to the woods. Derek got into bed and lay there, unable to sleep. After a while he heard a strange sound coming from outside his window, a sort of breathy, whistling sound.

29 *Presenting quotations*

If a quotation is as long as a complete line of poetry, or longer, separate it from your commentary by starting it on a new line and setting it in from the margin. Do not use quotation marks: setting the passage out, in its own space, does away with the need for them. When you resume your commentary start a new line again, beginning (unless you happen to be opening a new paragaph) against the left-hand margin.

> Macbeth is a good liar:
> > O! yet I do repent me of my fury,
> > That I did kill them.
>
> But Macduff, who has been watching him closely, is already suspicious.

In an examination you will not have time to quote long speeches, and you will not be expected to. If you want to indicate that you are referring to the whole of a speech, quote the opening phrase and put a row of dots after it:

> Othello addresses the Senators quietly and confidently:
> > Most potent, grave, and reverend signiors. . . .

If you quote two or more passages consecutively, put a row of dots after each one, to separate them:

> Othello often speaks of his past:
> > I fetch my life and being
> > From men of royal siege. . . .
> > Wherein I spake of most disastrous chances,

> Of moving accidents by flood and field. . . .
>   That handkerchief
> Did an Egyptian to my mother give. . . .

You can use a quotation to complete the sense of your own sentence. Put a dash (*not* a colon) to lead the reader's eye forward:

> Prospero describes how Antonio's ministers prepared –
> > A rotten carcass of a butt, not rigg'd,
> > Nor tackle, sail, nor mast.

> In a mood of happy anticipation Prospero tells Ariel to –
> >   bring a corollary
> > Rather than want a spirit.

You can also continue your own sentence into a quotation, and complete it after it. Again, put dashes, to lead the reader through the quotation:

> The contrast between Banquo and Macbeth is made plain at the beginning, when they meet the witches. While the gentle Banquo asks them mildly –
> >   Live you? or are you aught
> > That men may question?
> – the more aggressive Macbeth pushes forward and orders them to speak.

If a quotation is only a short one – a single word, perhaps, or a short phrase – introduce it into your own commentary by underlining it or by using quotation marks. (Underlining a word you write produces the equivalent, in print, of italics.)

> Shakespeare has peopled his island with strange creatures. There are apes that 'mow and chatter',

adders with 'cloven tongues', and elves that chase the ebbing tide across the sands 'with printless foot'.

Most quotations from prose works should be short extracts. You will gain nothing by memorizing a long passage, word for word, and setting it out in full in your examination answer. The purpose of including quotations in your answers is to support or illustrate your argument, not to show that you know them by heart.

Lawrence admires the fox. It is a 'lovely dog-fox in its prime'. It has a belly as 'white and soft as snow', a 'wonderful black-glinted brush', and a 'thick splendour of a tail'.

If you introduce a series of short quotations consecutively, separate them by putting dots between them:

Miranda expresses her wonder in simple words: 'a brave form . . . a thing divine . . . he's gentle'.

Simon keeps up a flow of banter: 'I wonder if there's any likelihood of dinner. . . . Now then, sir, there's a bird here waiting for you. . . . Here's something to make your hair curl.'

Brackets are useful:

Stephen remembered the girl's low voice (she 'murmured as if fascinated') and the way the boy staggered into the room under his load of coal.

Uncle Charles's efforts to stop the argument ('come now! . . . it's too bad surely') had no effect.

Othello restrains himself from dwelling on the topic ('No more of that') and turns to the last question that remains to be settled.

Gonzalo did not hear the words of the song that Ariel

sang in his ear ('While you here do snoring lie'), but he was aware of a strange 'humming'.

All titles must be quoted: that is, they must be either underlined or enclosed by quotation marks.

King Lear is a tragic play.

That is nonsense.

'King Lear' is a tragic play.

So too must all words that you refer to as words.

By and large is a meaningless phrase.

That is nonsense too.

'By and large' is a meaningless phrase.

30 Introducing quotations: doubling the quotation

A student will sometimes introduce a quotation in such a way that he has already quoted it before he has reached it. This practice produces an odd effect – as though the writer were implying: 'There! I've got *that* one in.'

> Chaucer adds the final touch to his description of the Summoner's ugliness by telling us that children were afraid of his face:
> Of his visage children were afeard.

> Chaucer adds the final touch to his description of the Summoner's ugliness by telling us that children were 'afeard' of his 'visage'.

> Brutus tells Cassius that his threats do not frighten him:
> There is no terror, Cassius, in thy threats.

> Brutus replies:
> There is no terror, Cassius, in thy threats.

> Keats longs for a drink of wine –
> O for a draught of vintage!

> Keats longs for a 'draught of vintage'.

> Romeo replies that he has the darkness of the night ('night's cloak') to hide him from Juliet's kinsmen.

> Romeo replies that he has 'night's cloak' to hide him from Juliet's kinsmen.

Lady Macbeth is afraid that her husband's nature is too kind:
    It is too full o' the milk of human kindness.

Lady Macbeth is afraid that her husband's nature is 'too full o' the milk of human kindness'.

The sword flashed in the moonlight –
    Made lightnings in the splendour of the moon.

The sword –
    Made lightnings in the splendour of the moon.

Now rewrite these passages in such a way as to eliminate the 'doubling'. In one of them it may be better to make the quotation flow continuously from the introductory sentence, instead of setting it out on a new line:

Ophelia's clothes (the Queen tells Laertes) spread wide in the water and bore her up, so that she seemed like a mermaid:
    And, mermaid-like, awhile they bore her up.

Caesar declares that he prefers to have fat, contented men about him, and that he distrusts Cassius because he is thin:
    Cassius has a lean and hungry look.

Lawrence describes how the mother kangaroo moves slowly away, almost like a ski-er:
    Goes off in slow sad leaps
    On the long flat skis of her legs.

Roy Campbell relates how he looked round and caught sight of the horses in the distance:
    And, turning, saw afar
    A hundred snowy horses unconfined.

31 Introducing quotations: failing to explain the context

A student will sometimes introduce a quotation too abruptly, without explaining the context:

> Prospero is a deeply imaginative man:
> The cloud-capp'd towers, the gorgeous palaces.

This practice often produces an odd effect too – as though the writer were just casually tossing out the quotation with an air of 'You know – all that jazz.'

> Prospero is a deeply imaginative man. On one occasion, for example, he has a majestic vision of some great civilization – of its 'cloud-capp'd towers' and its 'gorgeous palaces'.

> In the closing scenes of the play Macbeth's nerves and temper become frayed to breaking-point:
> > If thou speak'st false
> Upon the next tree shalt thou hang alive.

> In the closing scenes of the play Macbeth's nerves and temper become frayed to breaking-point. For example, when a messenger brings news that Birnam Wood has begun to move, Macbeth turns on him and threatens:
> > If thou speak'st false
> Upon the next tree shalt thou hang alive.

> Friar Laurence is a kindly, gentle-mannered man:

What early tongue so sweet saluteth me?

Friar Laurence is a kindly, gentle-mannered man. For example, when Romeo approaches him in the early morning and bids him 'good morrow', the Friar inquires mildly –

What early tongue so sweet saluteth me?

Othello has a majestic dignity:

Keep up your bright swords, for the dew will rust them.

Othello has a majestic dignity. He shows it, for example, in the early part of the play, when with one brief command he silences Brabantio and his followers:

Keep up your bright swords, for the dew will rust them.

32 Introducing quotations: the 'run-through'

When a sentence is continued into a quotation it must be joined to it in such a way that the sense runs through smoothly and logically and grammatically.

> Romeo is filled with wonder when he sees that –
> . . . here lies Juliet, and her beauty makes
> This vault a feasting presence full of light.

This is badly arranged: the run-through is neither smooth nor grammatical.

> Romeo is filled with wonder when he looks on Juliet.
> Her beauty, it seems to him, makes the vault a
> 'feasting presence full of light'.

> Antony begs Caesar's corpse to forgive him for being –
>
> . . . meek and gentle with these butchers.
> Thou art the ruins of the noblest man
> That ever lived in the tide of times.

The mistake here is not that the quotation has been badly joined to the sentence it completes, but that the second part of it has not been introduced at all.

> Antony begs Caesar's corpse to forgive him for being
> 'meek and gentle with these butchers'. He goes on to declare:
> Thou art the ruins of the noblest man
> That ever lived in the tide of times.

Here are some more examples:

> Caliban tells Stephano and Trinculo to –
> Be not afeard; the isle is full of noises,
> Sounds, and sweet airs, that give delight and hurt
> not.

> Caliban tells Stephano and Trinculo not to be
> 'afeard'. The island, he explains, is –
> . . . full of noises,
> Sounds, and sweet airs, that give delight and hurt
> not.

> Macbeth announces grimly that 'I have done the
> deed'.

> Macbeth announces grimly that he has 'done the
> deed'.

> Keats pictures autumn sitting by a cyder-press:
> Thou watchest the last oozings hours by hours.

> Keats pictures autumn sitting by a cyder-press and
> watching 'the last oozings hours by hours'.

> Ophelia bewails the fact that she –
> Now see that noble and most sovereign reason,
> Like sweet bells jangled, out of tune and harsh.

> Ophelia bewails the fact that she now sees –
> . . . that noble and most sovereign reason,
> Like sweet bells jangled, out of tune and harsh.

> Wordsworth then asks what song it is that the
> Highland girl is singing:
> Perhaps the plaintive numbers flow
> For old, unhappy, far-off things. . . .

> Wordsworth then asks what song it is that the
> Highland girl is singing, and he imagines that –

> Perhaps the plaintive numbers flow
> For old, unhappy, far-off things. . . .

Will you now re-shape these passages, and in each one make the run-through perfect. In three of them the quotation is set out on a new line. Possibly, in one or more of these, it may be better to make it flow continuously from the introductory sentence:

> The King envies all those poor and lowly people who can sleep peacefully because they are untroubled by affairs of state, quite different from –
> Uneasy lies the head that wears a crown.

> Antony, looking on the corpse, can hardly believe that –
> O mighty Caesar! dost thou lie so low?

> During a pause in the fighting Macbeth defiantly shouts out that 'I bear a charmed life'.

> Hardy humorously describes Gabriel Oak's smile as 'the corners of his mouth spread till they were within an unimportant distance of his ears'.

> Ted Hughes describes the otter as being –
> With webbed feet and long ruddering tail
> And a round head like an old tomcat.

General exercises

These exercises consist of passages in which every sentence contains various faults of style. After the sentences there are numbers, referring to the sections in the text of the book. You should study each sentence, try to work out what is wrong with it, and then rewrite it. If you are uncertain, you can refer to the section indicated by the number. Here you will find an explanation, in general terms, of what is wrong. In this way, by working through the whole exercise, you can turn a badly written passage into a well written one.

You should not be deterred from doing a particular exercise by the fact that you are unfamiliar with the work of literature on which it is based. These are exercises in style, and a knowledge of the subject-matter is not necessary.

Exercises 1–12 relate to the O-level English Language examination.

Exercises 13–24 relate to the O-level English Literature examination.

Exercises 25–36 relate to the A-level English Literature examination.

Exercises 1–12: General essays, O-level English Language examination

Exercise 1

It can be said that shop windows definitely look their best in December. 6.5. At this time of year, when the weather is just awful, their glitter drives away the darkness and gloom of winter and expresses the gay spirit of Christmas. 22. 18. 16.

After Christmas the sales begin and the displays are abandoned and all the old stock is brought out. 2. The sales spirit is absolutely nothing like the Christmas spirit, for all the magic has completely gone and an atmosphere of cheap trickery somehow prevails. 5. 16. 6. Most of the goods are definitely shoddy, but many people are so tempted by the price reductions that they are tricked into buying the goods. 5. 13.

After the sales the spring season. 8. At this time of year the shop windows are simply filled with greeting-cards, chocolate eggs, and other goods connected with Easter, and perhaps the most spring-like windows are those of the gown shops, for they have fantastic brides' and brides-maids' dresses in them. 22. 2. 20.

Soon spring merges into summer – so slowly and gradually that we hardly notice the change. 16. It could be said that summer is a rather bright time for the shops. 6. 5. The windows soon look so different, for summer dresses, swimsuits, and sports wear of all kinds now begin to dominate the windows. 10. 13.

Finally, as autumn gets near, the airy lightness of summer fades from the shop windows and winter's heavy look takes its place and thick coats and woollens are all that matter now. 23. 2. This is the very dullest time of year in the high streets, for summer's brightness has been completely and utterly forgotten and the gaiety of Christmas is still such a long way off. 5. 16. 10. The shops, at this time of year are definitely at their emptiest. 27. 5. But before long, however, the appearance of these shops begins to change again. 16. 13. Soon the very first Christmas cards are being put on display, and as we walk past the windows we seem to realize that once more the windows are preparing to clothe themselves in their nicest dress of all. 5. 6. 13. 18.

It can be said that in these various ways as the year goes round, the shop windows reflect the season. 6. 27. These windows even reflect life itself. 13. Like the windows, sometimes dull and sometimes bright. 8.

Exercise 2

If there were no oceans on the earth all vegetation would definitely die, and the human race would just not be able to carry on. 5. 22. 20. It is the oceans that make the world fruitful and rich and fertile. 16. Without the oceans the world would be as cold as the moon or as dried up and barren as the Sahara. 13. 13. 16.

Also the sea helps to make life so much more thrilling and exciting. 7. 10. 16. Most people know something about the marvellous voyages of discovery that were made in the past, and pretty well everyone must have heard of the achievements in our own time of people like Clare Francis. 18. 20. 21. But, although people have sailed over all the oceans of the world, and have mapped them out there are still great mysteries yet to be explored in the depths of the oceans. 27. 16. 13. It can be said that exploring the bottom of the sea is an adventure as good as exploring outer space. 6. 18.

The sea also makes our lives more beautiful and many poems have been written about it, for the sea is by far the most majestic sight in nature. 2. 13. It is not surprising that people just love to spend their holidays on its shores, so that they may be strengthened by its pure air, and calmed and rested by its peacefulness and serenity. 22. 16. 16. In all these respects the sea is definitely man's friend. 5.

Yet the sea can also be said to be man's enemy. 6. The sea is man's enemy not only when he sails on it and faces the angry fury of its storms, but also when man is dwelling peacefully on the firm land. 13. 13. 16. 13. On many occasions in the past high tides have simply battered their way through sea walls and caused awful disasters. 22. 18. At such times the sea is a ruthless foe that shows no pity. 16.

Exercise 3

In the London Zoo most of the wild animals are kept in small cages and this is not a satisfactory arrangement for it means that the animals can do no more than just prowl backwards and forwards. 2. 13. 16. It is a sad and tragic thing to see powerful animals restricted to a space no bigger than a small yard. 16. 21. But there is one advantage, in the London Zoo it is possible for visitors to go ever so near to the animals. 28. 10. Often visitors can go to within a few feet of the animals, with only the bars to mark the dividing line. 13. 13. It is a good experience, at this close range, to see the lions being fed, and every day at feeding time crowds always collect in front of the cages to watch. 18. 16. This sight would simply never be seen if the animals were kept in more open conditions and were not kept in relatively small cages. 22. 16.

In the London Zoo some of the strongest and most

powerful animals live in cages of this kind. 16. Lions, tigers, leopards, and other large wild cats. 8. But some other animals have got quite a bit more freedom. 23. 20. The polar bears, for example, have got a swimming pool and a rocky slope, arranged to resemble the natural surroundings of the bears; and the penguins, which live in ever such a big enclosure, have slides and steps to keep them amused. 23. 13. 10. Some of the large tame animals, too, have quite a bit of freedom, for they are often allowed to wander round uncaged. 20. Many of the birds live in the aviary that was thought up by Lord Snowdon, and its vast height gives them almost complete and total freedom to fly about as they please, and its trees and shrubs make it possible for these birds to construct their nests in natural surroundings. 20. 2. 16. 13. 19.

It can safely be said that the most popular thing in the London Zoo is the children's corner. 6. 21. Tame animals are kept in the children's corner. 13. Rabbits, mice, hens and donkeys. 8. Very good entertainments are held for the children, such as the chimpanzees' tea-party, which always gets lots of laughs. 18. 23. 20. Also the children can have rides on elephants and camels, and watch monkeys doing tricks, and enjoy other things of that kind. 7. 21.

Exercise 4

I know a person who has a thing about wigs. 20. He regards wigs as a form of disguise, and he thinks that people who wear wigs are cheats or frauds. 13. 13. 16. Now I definitely disagree with this view really strongly. 5. 5. One might just as well make out that clothes are a form of disguise. 20. Or cosmetics, or elaborate hairstyles. 8. All through history human beings have tried to make themselves look nice by getting themselves up in various ways. 18. 20. They have dressed themselves in wonderful clothes, they have placed incredible crowns and hats on their heads, they have worn marvellous jewels on their fingers, and over their hair these human beings have put wigs. 18. 18. 18. 13.

The idea of wigs for men is a big laugh for some people. 20. A handsome young man at one moment, with thick black hair, and a few seconds later a bald-headed grandfather. 8. It is so easy to laugh at other people. 10. In fact, men who wear wigs do so because they tend to be rather sensitive on their baldness. 6. 5. 15. A wig is a really marvellous asset to a bald man who is worried or anxious about his appearance, for a wig enables this man to face life with confidence. 5. 18. 16. 13. 13. He need have absolutely no fear that anyone will deduce that he is wearing one. 5. 19. Most modern male wigs are definitely completely undetectable, for these wigs are made of real hair and each one is cleverly and skilfully designed to suit one single individual person. 5. 13. 16. 16.

There is a wide variety and range of female wigs. 16. Some are made of imitation hair, and some of real hair, and you can get them in lots of different colours. 23. 20. The imitation-hair ones are not really as good as the real-hair ones, for the imitation-hair ones have to be worn always in the one style. 5. 13. Real-hair wigs on the other hand, can be set in absolutely any style that is wanted. 27. 5. A woman will do better therefore, to choose one made of real hair, even though it may knock her back a bit. 27. 20.

Exercise 5

Some people are dead against space travel, and they maintain that it is just absurd to spend millions of dollars on trying to reach the planets when this world is in such a mess. 20. 2. 22. 20. These people think that the money should be spent instead on feeding the great numbers of unfortunate and unhappy people who are starving. 13. 16.

Also they argue that it is ridiculous to suppose that man will achieve any success in the rest of the universe when man is not even capable of organizing things properly on this earth. 7. 13. 21.

These arguments are bad, for they do not take into account the fact that simply enormous sums of money are spent on achieving objects which are so much less worthwhile than space travel. 18. 22. 10. Armaments, for example, which definitely help no one, and which threaten the existence of the human race. 5. 8. Also, if space travel were discontinued there is definitely no guarantee that the money saved would be spent on helping to feed the hungry or the starving. 7. 5. 16.

People who carry on about space travel also forget that a love of adventure is a basic thing in human nature. 20. 21. Throughout the entire course of history men have sought to explore the unknown, and to face big challenges, and this spirit of adventure has been one of the main things driving civilization forward. 16. 18. 21. It inspired the great Elizabethan sailors of the past to sail the oceans and seas in search of unknown lands. 16. 16. It inspired Livingstone to make an exploration of the jungle, and Scott to try to be the first man to get to the South Pole. 25. 23. Today it is without doubt inspiring men to journey to the planets. 6. It is a spirit that will never be destroyed or crushed. 16. For when man has colonized the planets, he will go on from there to reach the nearer stars, and after he has reached the nearer stars man will journey yet further still. 13. 13. 16. People who think that this marvellous adventure is a waste of money do not understand what makes human beings tick. 18. 20. They cannot see that our lives would be ever so dreary if we did not have things like space travel to think about. 10. 21.

Exercise 6

When we think of the beauty of England we tend to picture pretty villages, ancient old cities, and quiet meadows and hills. 6. 16. This kind of thing gradually grew up over many hundreds of years. 21. 16. In the past, whenever a town or a village was built by men, or whenever a road was laid out by them, they made England a more beautiful place. 26. 26. The houses, which were built of local stone really blended with the landscape and merged into it, and the villages without doubt added life to a countryside that would otherwise have been dull and boring. 27. 5. 16. 6. 16. The roads, too, though they may have been awful to ride along, looked nice, because their surface consisted not of tarmac but of the local soil of the area. 18. 18. 16.

Today all this beauty is disappearing so fast, for this beauty belongs wholly and entirely to a bygone age. 10. 13. 16. Pretty nearly everything that man builds today makes England an uglier and less beautiful place. 20. 16. Rotten-looking houses are built, and they are laid out in strips along straight roads that have just no character at all. 20. 22. The bricks which the houses are built of are not made on the spot and haven't got any relationship with the environment around them. 20. 23. 16. The new roads are horrible carriage-ways that are laid across the countryside with a complete and utter disregard for its beauty. 18. 16. They just slice their way through beautiful patches of lovely downland, or through previously quiet villages, bringing noise and dirt and din in their wake. 22. 16. 16.

The future does not look good. 18. With every year that passes more and more of England's beauty and charm is being simply destroyed. 16. 22. Narrow, picturesque streets being widened so that the traffic can get down them, and a network of concrete roads gradually being extended to cover even the most remote and isolated country districts. 23. 16. 8. Nevertheless, when saying things like this we should remember that all this can be looked at from a different point of view. 23. 21. 12. A good lot of poverty has disappeared from our cities, and there are better standards of health and less illness. 20. 16. Also, a good bit of ignorant narrow-minded superstition has been cleared away from country districts, and all over England people are better educated and less ignorant than they used to be in former times. 7. 20. 16. 16. 16. But there is a price to be paid for these things, the loss of England's beauty. 21. 28.

Exercise 7

Let us first consider the question as to what the advantages of television are. 4. Old people, unquestionably, find television a blessing. 13. Many of them, because they are maybe too old or too sick to be able to leave their homes in the evenings, would feel really lost without television. 20. 5. 13. It can also be said that television is useful as a means of communication. 6. Before the invention of broadcasting many parts of England tended to be cut off and isolated from the rest of the country, and the lives of a not inconsiderable proportion of the population tended to be narrow and ignorant. 6. 16. 19. 6. This situation has now quite definitely changed, for today the news bulletins that regularly appear every day on the television keep people in touch with things. 5. 5. 16. 21. Finally, there is no doubt that television is really useful as a means of education. 6. 5. All sorts of educational things get shown, not only to classes in schools but also to adults too. 21. 23. 16.

Television however, has quite a few disadvantages to it as well, and one of these disadvantages is that television makes people lazy. 27. 20. 15. 2. 13. 13. Today, by just turning a switch, and doing nothing more than that, one can enjoy a play or a film in the comfort and luxury of one's home. 16. 16. But the edge of the enjoyment will have got blunted, for television has dulled and deadened the excitement of pleasures of this kind by making these pleasures too easily available. 23. 16. 13. Before it was thought up people had to take the trouble to go out for their entertainment. 20. If people wanted to see a film they had to be ready at a certain fixed time, and then get a bus or a train, and when they got to the cinema they perhaps had to queue. 13. 16. 23. 23. Going to the theatre in those days was a still more elaborate thing, for going to the theatre might even have involved dressing up in evening gear. 21. 13. 20. In all cases, before television was invented, people really had to go to quite a bit of trouble to find their entertainment, and the efforts they had to put in made them enjoy it so much more. 5. 20. 10.

Exercise 8

Many of the sentences in this passage are too long; separate statements, that should have been expressed in separate sentences, have been run together.

There is a stretch of coast in North Devon that has a very special place in my affections and it lies between Ilfracombe, to the north, and the very picturesque village of Croyde, to the south. 5. 2. 5. It is an especially beautiful coast because it has not been spoilt by modern developments because the National Trust has bought large areas of it. 14. I always go there every August, and I stay in a small farmhouse in the valley of Lee and at that time of year the countryside is always so beautiful, for then the bindweed and the mallow flowers are out, and the corn is such a deep yellow, and the cliffs are simply covered with the withered flowers of sea-pinks. 16. 2. 10. 10. 22. Sometimes, in August, the weather can be just great. 22. 20. If it is, the whole of this bit of England becomes really full of the lazy, sleepy, drowsy atmosphere of late summertime. 20. 5. 16.

This coastal countryside is fertile and extremely varied in character and never monotonous, thickly wooded valleys being interspersed with very wide sweeps of grass-covered hills, and these in turn making a big contrast from the stretches of sand that thread their way rather like a yellow ribbon between the sea and the cliffs. 16. 2. 5. 18. 15. 5. A person can find complete and total solitude on some of these green western hills, for these hills are the haunt of only sheep and gulls and no other creatures. 16. 13. 16. There are hardly any works of man to be seen, though a few buildings are scattered here and there, a farmhouse perhaps, or the grey ruin of a cottage, and there are gates and stiles, but these are all made of local materials and so they merge and blend into the scenery in a very natural way. 2. 28. 16. 5. Indeed, in certain lights, the stone farmsteads in a way look more similar to boulders than to a group of buildings. 6. 19.

The cliff-sides are even lonelier than the hills, rearing hundreds of feet above the shore and stretching along it rather in the manner of a gigantic, jagged curtain. 2. 5. 19. These rock-faces are a world in themselves, absolutely cut off from civilization and not connected with it in any way. 5. 16. The very things that make them inaccessible to man, their very great height, their roughness, their nearness to the sea, make them an ideal and perfect home for the gulls and the kittiwakes and these white birds are the sole masters here and they alone rule over them. 21. 28. 5. 16. 2. 16.

Exercise 9

Several colons and dashes are needed, if this passage is to be properly punctuated.

It can be said that each of the four different seasons can be associated with a different time of life. 6. 16. There is really no doubt as to what age spring is associated with, it belongs to the young. 5. 28. All those aspects of life that form a part of it, the lambs in the fields, the young fledgelings in their nests, the buds that push and thrust their way forward, remind one of youth. 28. 16. 16. A time for young people to fall in love, and to think of marrying and having kids of their own. 20. 8. Old people may love the spring, but they are not a part of it, but they love it because of the memories it brings of the times when they were young. 14.

Summer can in a way be said to belong to both the young and the old. 6. 6. Young people can take full advantage of all that summer offers, they can swim, do a bit of sunbathing, and take part in all kinds of sports. 13. 28. 20. Old people too, can enjoy it, for just as soon as the first warm days of June are here, they can get in the sun. 27. 22. 23. It must be very nice, if you are an old person, and have just endured a rather long winter, to sit outside and lap up the sunshine. 18. 5. 20.

Autumn is really rather more closely associated with the old than with the young, for at this time of year the whole of nature can be said to be dying. 5. 5. 6. A season of serene and peaceful calm, a time for remembering with quiet and thankful gratitude, the happiness and pleasure that the summer brought. 16. 16. 16. 8. It is definitely not a time for looking forward, for the spring seems so far away. 5. 10. That is why autumn belongs most especially to those whose lives are nearly over and finished. 16. 16.

Winter brings one word to mind straight off, Christmas.

20. 28. Christmas draws people of all ages together, for Christmas has one special thing that sets it apart from the other times of the year, it is the season of good will. 13. 21. 28. On Christmas Day young and old join together, and the same meals are shared by them, and the same games are played, and they sit in the same circle round the Christmas tree, and it is a time when all differences of age are put out of mind and forgotten. 26. 26. 2. 16.

Exercise 10

As in exercise 8, many of the sentences in this passage are too long; separate statements, which should have been expressed in separate sentences, have been run together.

Aunt Betty dresses quietly and with simplicity, and for most of the time she usually wears a plain grey blouse and a skirt of some dull colour, so dull that it is rather hard to remember exactly what it is. 25. 2. 16. 28. 5. When you first see her face you immediately notice one thing in particular, her slanting eyelids, and her eyes are almost completely hidden behind them. 21. 28. 2. But although they are hidden you tend to feel that there must be a kindly twinkle in them although you can only guess what is in their depths. 6. 14. Aunt Betty's most characteristic appearance is when she is busy in her garden. 11. When working there she always wears a chip-straw hat, her usual grey clothes that she generally wears, and a pair of goloshes and just nothing in the world makes her happier than doing those little things in the garden that require patience rather than hard or strenuous physical effort. 16. 2. 22. 21. 16.

It would not be pretended by anyone that Aunt Betty is a pretty woman, her appearance in fact being dowdy. 26. 2. But, strange though it may seem, it is really almost a compliment to describe her in this way, and she herself, I feel absolutely sure, would not get annoyed if she over-heard the description. 5. 5. 23. For this is part of her character. 12. The very pleasantness of Aunt Betty's whole outlook and of her whole way of life lies in the fact that she is self-effacing and never pushes herself forward. 13. 16.

My aunt has some odd hobbies, one of them being an interest in astrology, and every month she regularly buys magazines about this subject, and in her sitting-room there is a whole shelf-full of books devoted to this subject. 2. 2. 16. 13. Also she is so fussy about food, for she is a vegetarian in the very strictest sense of the word, who will never touch anything that could possibly have got any meat in it. 7. 10. 5. 23. But one point must be made very clear in this connection, she never tries to shove her ideas at you. 5. 28. 20. In fact she has fine, broad-minded views and opinions about life in general, and you never hear Aunt Betty objecting, for example, to modern gear, or moaning on about the behaviour of the young people of today. 16. 2. 13. 20. 20. If the world had more people like her in it one feels, the world would be a better place. 27. 13.

Exercise 11

This passage is full of empty words and repetitive expressions.

It can be stated that in some ways advertising is one of the bad and undesirable things in modern life. 6. 16. 21. Many advertisements, especially those dealing with bodily or physical requirements, somehow lower the dignity of life and pull it down. 16. 6. 16. The advertisements on food, for example, lend such an exaggeration to the simple pleasure of eating that they make it seem an unpleasant thing. 15. 25. 21. Those that deal with soaps or scents make it seem that a woman's fortunes in love are completely and utterly dependent on which brand that woman gets. 16. 13. 23. This sort of stuff definitely cheapens life. 20. 5.

Also there is no doubt that advertising plays on the ignorance of people and makes use of it. 7. 6. 16. Some advertisements con people into buying goods that they simply do not need, and others make very false claims about products. 20. 22. 5. Some advertisers really go to town about the goods they are trying to sell – for example, really absurd claims tend to be made, in very far-fetched language, about the powers of certain washing powders. 5. 20. 5. 6. 5. Indeed, so much deception has been carried on that the government has introduced certain rules and regulations to counteract this deception and put a stop to it. 20. 16. 13. 16.

Finally, many advertisements can without question be said to be ugly. 6. 6. There is really nothing more awful than a hoarding with an ugly poster on it. 5. 18. The colours are likely to be just terrible, the drawing will consist of crude lines that have no delicacy, and these two things will be exaggerated by the very great size of the poster. 22. 18. 16. 21. 5. A rather large part in creating the ugliness of the modern world has been played by beastly hoardings of this kind. 5. 26. 18.

We will next consider the question as to whether advertising has any favourable aspects. 4. It undoubtedly and quite certainly has. 16. Many advertisements can be said to be dignified and honest notices, providing the public at large with useful and valuable information. 6. 16. 16. Others take the form of very decorative paintings that brighten up the drabness and gloom of some street or station. 5. 16. Finally, advertising makes a positive and useful contribution to life in another way, it provides revenue. 16. 28. Commercial television, for example, is financed solely and entirely by the revenue from advertising, and most newspapers are sold as cheaply as they are, and are not dearer, because they get a steady and continuous revenue from the same source. 16. 16. 23. 16.

Exercise 12

Several colons and dashes are needed, if this passage is to be properly punctuated.

It is true to say that the major proportion of the music we hear today is mechanically reproduced. 6. 19. We hear an awful lot of it, indeed, some people probably spend most of their waking hours within reach of the sound of this music. 20. 28. 13. Because we hear so much of it we really tend to take little notice of it because often, while it is being played, we are engaged in some task or other that absorbs our attention. 5. 6. 14. This situation has brought about a new attitude towards music, it has made people indifferent towards music. 28. 13.

Now music is definitely the only really and truly noble sound that man can produce. 5. 16. Other creatures, one might make mention of seagulls, for example, or nightingales, or even wolves, have naturally beautiful cries. 28. 25. But there is just not one bit of beauty in the ordinary sounds of human communication. 22. 20. That is why music has always been such a big thing for man, for by means of this art of his he can beat the beauty of all other sounds on earth. 18. 21. 20. It is therefore not surprising that in previous ages, prior to this age of ours, people always stopped to have a listen when they heard music. 16. 25. To our forefathers it would not have been just a mere sound coming out of a mechanical device, it would have been a sound produced by a group of people who had got together in order to play or sing in harmony. 16. 28. 23. But today, as a result of the changes brought about by the modern inventions of this age, it is no longer valued any more at its true worth. 16. 16.

On the other hand, the invention of mechanically reproduced music has brought with it one advantage of not inconsiderable proportions, it has made it possible for us to preserve the sounds made by great musicians. 19. 28. Some idea of the importance of this advantage can be formed by us if we try to see the thing from the point of view of future generations. 26. 21. They will not wonder what the music of our age sounded like, they will hear this music. 28. 13.

Exercises 13–24: O-level English Literature examination

Exercise 13

Macbeth is definitely a play about darkness. 5. All the most dramatic things take place after night has fallen, or in a rather dim light. 21. 5. The night on which Duncan is stabbed and murdered is particularly black, and its sinister darkness receives several mentions. 16. 25. Lady Macbeth calls on it to clothe itself in the thick smoke of hell:

And pall thee in the dunnest smoke of hell. 30.

She wants this night to be just as black as it can be so that –

Nor heaven peep through the blanket of the dark. 13. 22. 32.

When Banquo walks out into the courtyard, after twelve, there was just no light at all. 9. 22. We know that there is none because Banquo says to his son that heaven's 'candles' had all been put out. 13. 23. 9. Later, he too was murdered under the cover of darkness. 9. The murderers strike Banquo down at a time when all travellers are hurrying fast to gain the 'timely inn' because the light is failing. 13. 16. Another dark scene is when Macbeth consults the witches. 11. Macbeth meets the witches in a dark and gloomy cavern, and while Macbeth speaks to them a storm rages angrily. 13. 13. 16. 13. 16. Finally, in the scene with Lady Macbeth sleep-walking, the only light in the room is just the taper Lady Macbeth is carrying. 15. 16. 13.

On numerous occasions during the course of the play there are many flashes of light, and the contrasts they introduce make the darkness seem more. 19. 16. 18. The dagger that Macbeth saw in a vision, when he was waiting to murder Duncan, gleams and flashes in the dark court-yard of the palace. 9. 9. 16. Again, when the three murderers were waiting for Banquo outside the palace gates, one of the murderers points towards the west and remarks that still –

The west yet glimmers with some streaks of day. 9. 13. 32.

In the scene in the witches' cavern flashes of lightning piercing the blackness and lighting it up, and the flames under the cauldron making a patch of really vivid light. 16. 5. 8. Finally, in the sleep-walking scene, we can imagine how the taper which Lady Macbeth is holding must light up Lady Macbeth's white face, and set it in sharp contrast from the darkness that surrounds it on all sides. 13. 15. 16.

Exercise 14

In the first verse of the ode 'To Autumn' the mellowing of summer is described by Keats, and everything is at its most fruitful. 26. 2. The vines are simply loaded with grapes, the cottage-trees were bowed down with apples, and the bees were still plentifully supplied with many flowers. 22. 9. 9. 16. The description of the bees is especially good, for the sound of such words as 'summer', 'brimmed', and 'clammy' puts across their quiet humming. 18. 20. The scene as a whole somehow has an atmosphere of quiet and peaceful calm. 6. 16. There is no movement, and no living creatures are brought in except just the bees. 20. 16.

The second verse is very much more fanciful. 5. Autumn is personified by Keats, and he pictures her as being present as a watcher while the harvest was being gathered. 26. 9. She is seen in a granary –

Sitting careless on a granary floor. . . .

or watching a cyder-press –

> Thou watchest the last oozings hours by hours. 30.
> 32.

There is not a terrific lot of detail in this verse. 20. Instead of describing a real scene Keats makes up a dreamy picture of the spirit of autumn. 20. 20.

In the last verse he switches back to detailed description. 20. But the scene Keats describes now, in contrast to the earlier one, definitely has some sound and movement to it. 13. 5. 15. In the first verse all we got was the quiet humming of the bees, but now we hear quite a few different sounds. 23. 20. We hear the 'loud bleat' of the lambs, and we catch the sound of –

> . . . with treble soft.
> The red-breast whistles from a garden-croft. 32.

Faintly, too, if we listen carefully –

> And gathering swallows twitter in the skies. 32.

The mood of this verse is sad and mournful, and there is definitely a suggestion of death in many of the lines. 16. 5. This sadness of mood is added to by some of the sounds. 24. For example, words such as 'wailful', 'mourn', 'borne', with their long vowels, bring across Keats's mood of sorrow and regret perfectly. 20. 16. Finally, in the reference to the gathering swallows, there is a cunning suggestion that the winter is only just round the corner. 20. 20.

Exercise 15

There is no doubt that a good bit of the charm of 'Afterwards' lies in its simplicity. 6. 20. Will people remember him, Hardy says, after he is dead and gone, and, if they do, will they associate him with what he loved and cherished when he was alive? 23. 16. 16. This simple question is the basic theme in the poem. 16. 15.

Hardy starts off by thinking of the leaves of May. 20. He calls them 'delicate-filmed as new-spun silk', and he wonders if anyone will remember how closely and carefully he observed these leaves. 23. 16. 13. Then Hardy's thoughts turn away from the spring, and an 'upland' scene is pictured by him. 13. 26. It is dusk, and Hardy gets a glimpse of the 'dewfall hawk' as it alights on the 'wind-warped thorn'. 13. 23. Its flight is described by him as being like 'an eyelid's soundless blink', and by means of this simile he puts over a good impression of the complete silence of its movement. 26. 20. 18. Next, he pictures a warm summer night ('mothy and warm') when hedgehogs can be seen about:

> When the hedgehog travels furtively over the lawn.
> 30. 30.

'Furtively' is a good word, for it brings over to the reader the idea that these animals are always afraid, and in the lines that follow Hardy thinks of the efforts he has made throughout his life to protect and defend 'innocent creatures' of this kind. 18. 20. 16. Then he imagines a winter's sky simply full of stars, and he remembers how often he has contemplated the mystery of the heavens and wondered about it. 22. 16. Finally, he remembers his way of noting even the smallest and most minute details. 16. Hardy had often noticed it seems, how when a bell was being tolled a passing breeze would cut off the sound for a moment:

> A crossing breeze cuts a pause in its outrollings. 13.
> 27. 30.

When his own funeral bell rings, he says to himself, will

people remember how observant he used to be in former times? 23. 16.

The poem definitely has an unusual rhythm to it, for though it is regularly rhymed the poem has no regular metre. 5. 15. 13. The lines are long, and their length seems to have been brought about and determined not so much by a fixed or regular rhythmical pattern as by the natural flow of Hardy's thoughts. 16. 16. This looseness of metre has a good effect on the character of the poem as a whole, for this metre makes us feel that these are definitely not the thoughts of a poet, but those of a plain, simple, ordinary man. 18. 13. 5. 16.

Exercise 16

In the earlier scenes Lady Macbeth definitely shows lots more determination than her husband. 5. 20. Just as soon as she hears that Duncan is coming, she makes up her mind that he's got to be murdered that night. 22. 23. Her only fear is that her husband, whose nature, she knows is too full of 'the milk of human kindness' will not be up to the job. 27. 27. 20.

Macbeth's first words, when he gets to the castle and meets his wife, are to tell his wife that Duncan is on his way. 23. 13. His wife asks him, with a tone of voice full of meaning, when the King expects to leave. 13. 15. He replies 'tomorrow', and then, as an afterthought, he says 'as he purposes'. 23. His wife is absolutely thrilled by the hint lying behind Macbeth's words, and she exclaims confidently that the sun will never see that tomorrow –

O never
Shall sun that morrow see. 5. 13. 30.

We next see Macbeth, in the evening, standing quite alone in one of the rooms of the castle, talking to himself. 5.

20. Macbeth had left Duncan and the other guests, who are still at supper, because his conscience is bothering him. 13. 9. 20. The murder might have bad consequences, he says to himself. 18. 23. Also, he reflects, Duncan is his kinsman and his guest, and he is a king who bears his high office meekly:

Hath borne his faculties so meek. 7. 30.

Lady Macbeth then enters the room, tense with nervousness and anxiety. 16. She asks her husband very angrily why he walked out on his guests. 5. 20. He does not answer her question, but instead he expresses at once the thing that is uppermost in his mind, he tells her that he has decided not to commit the murder. 21. 28. She then accuses him of being a coward, knowing that he despises this, and that he will go to absolutely any lengths to prove that he was not one. 12. 5. 9. He begs her to be silent and not say any more, but she ignores his plea and goes on to explain her plan, which is to frame the two chamberlains. 16. 20. Macbeth, really fascinated by the cleverness and simplicity of the idea caves in. 5. 27. 20. He is absolutely amazed at his wife's lack of womanly feeling and tenderness. 5. 16.

Exercise 17

An atmosphere of death hangs around some of the scenes in the Pardoner's tale. 20. The scene in the inn, for example. 8. Very weird and in a way really quite frightening. 5. 6. 5. 5. 8. As the rioters were sitting drinking, a bell was heard by them being rung in front of a dead corpse. 26. 16. This corpse was the corpse of a man who had just died only that very night, and it was being taken to its grave. 13. 9. 16. A 'privy thief' called Death had turned up in the tavern, where the man was sitting drunk, and had stabbed him to the heart:

And with his spear he smote his heart in two. 20. 30.

Death, it seems, was apparently very active in the country-side at that time, for the innkeeper says to the rioters how it had recently brought about the killing of all the inhabitants of a nearby village little more than a mile away. 16. 23. 25. 16.

The scene in which the rioters meet up with the old man is in a way even more sinister still. 20. 6. 16. A definitely weird figure. 5. 8. He is so very old, and every part of his body, except just his face, is tightly wrapped. 10. 16. He says to the rioters how he longs for death, and how all the time he continually taps on the ground in the hope that Mother Earth will receive him into a grave. 23. 16. But Mother Earth will not grant him his request, and for this reason, the old man informs the rioters,

For which full pale and welked is my face. 13. 13. 19. 32.

The Pardoner makes this scene even better still by setting it against a real background. 18. 16. The rioters meet the old man just as they are about to –

Right as they would have trodden over a stile. 32.

A 'crooked' lane leads away into the distance, and at the end of this lane a grove of trees. 13. 8. A touch of realism is added to the story by these things, and at the same time they add to the strangeness of the atmosphere. 26. 21. 24.

Exercise 18

The poem starts off sadly, for Keats has been listening to the nightingale, and the beauty of the nightingale's song has made him feel that ordinary life is awful. 20. 13. 18. He contemplates the world of men and calls it a place of 'palsy' and 'leaden-eyed despairs'. 23. He simply longs for a 'draught of vintage' that will enable him to get away from its 'fever'. 22. 23. Then, with the help of the power of poetry ('on the viewless wings of Poesy'), he transports himself, in his imagination, into the wonderful forest of the nightingale. 30. 18.

For a time Keats wanders through the dim depths of this forest – 'through verdurous gloom and winding mossy ways'. 30. Although he could not see the flowers at his feet he names a whole lot of them, because he can guess what they are because he can smell their fragrance. 9. 20. 14. He talks about the hawthorn, for example, and the violets, and the 'coming musk-rose'. 20. But he somehow seemed to be aware that he could enjoy this beautiful world for a short while only and that the aches and pains of life must return, for he reflects that if he were to die now he would never have to go back to them again. 6. 9. 9. 16. 16.

As his dream begins to fade, Keats gives quite a bit of thought to the question of death, reflecting to himself that if he were now to 'cease upon the midnight' the nightingale would still carry on singing, just as it is now singing long after the death of those who lived many centuries ago ('in ancient days'). 20. 2. 20. 30. Then one single word, 'forlorn', like a mournful bell, smashes his dream up. 16. 20. He bids the nightingale 'adieu' and concludes rather sadly that the imagination cannot fool a person for long. 5. 20.

Exercise 19

A lack of dignity is one of the faults that spoil this passage. Many of the expressions are colloquial and quite out of place.

Antony's opening words are pretty quiet, and in a way even apologetic. 20. 6. He speaks to the citizens respectfully, saying 'gentle Romans'. 23. If Caesar was ambitious, he tells them –

And grievously hath Caesar answered it. 32.

He then begins to start up doubts in their minds as to whether Caesar really was ambitious. 20. But Brutus he points out, maintains that he was, and Brutus is definitely an honourable man. 27. 5. After carrying on a bit longer about the honesty of Brutus, he suddenly puts on an act of breaking down, as though overcome with grief and sorrow. 20. 20. 20. 16. The citizens, seeing his grief, get pretty emotional. 23. 20.

Getting back to his speech, Antony brings up the subject of Caesar's will. 23. 20. If the people knew what was in this will, he cries out, they would definitely want to kiss 'dead Caesar's wounds'. 13. 5. But, says Antony, he's got no intention of reading out this will. 23. 23. 13. His reason for refusing, he says to the citizens, is that it would work them up too much. 23. 20. Also, he continues, those who killed Caesar are 'honourable men', and he must not stir up anger against these men. 7. 13. The citizens then shout out that Caesar's murderers were wicked villains, and they say they want to hear the will. 9. 16. 23.

Antony steps down among the people and gets more intimate in his attitude. 23. If they've got any tears he tells them, they really must shed them now. 23. 27. 5. He points to the places in Caesar's cloak where the daggers went in, and in particular he keeps on about the wound made by Brutus. 20. 20. Then he gets a climax by throwing the cloak aside and revealing Caesar's body. 23. This act rouses the crowd to a pitch of absolutely furious rage. 5. 16.

It can be stated that at this point Antony might well have left the mob to get on with it, but he is still not satisfied, however. 6. 20. 16. The conspirators, he points out, are quite clever speakers, and they could bring up sound reasons for killing Caesar. 5. 20. He himself, he declares, is not a smart talker, but a plain, blunt man who hadn't got any gimmicks. 20. 9. 23. 20. If he had the talking powers of Brutus, he continues, he would make such a terrific speech that the stones of Rome would simply rise up and mutiny. 20. 18. 22.

The citizens are now really furious. 5. So furious that Antony can hardly hold them back. 8. But he manages to restrain them a bit longer by reminding them that they have not yet heard the will and then he reads it to them. 20. 2. As they listen they become roused to a pitch of furious anger, and before he has even got through to the end they rush off, just determined to burn down the houses of the conspirators:

> And with the brands of fire the traitors' houses. 16. 23. 22. 30.

Exercise 20

This is another passage that suffers from a lack of dignity.

Sir Toby is not perhaps the sort of chap we would like to have as a friend. 20. Nevertheless, he is amusing, and not boring, and his faults are all on the surface and not hidden away. 16. 16. He is completely and utterly unrepentant about his drinking, he intends to go on with his drinking he declares, 'as long as there is drink in Illyria'. 16. 28. 13. 27. His liking, too, for what Olivia describes as 'fruitless pranks' definitely tends to make him a bit of a character. 5. 6. 20. For example, when we see Sir Toby arranging a duel for Cesario, and at the same time making sure of pulling a fast one on Sir Andrew, we cannot help thinking that he is rather a laugh. 13. 20. 20.

But Sir Toby's character has got more in it than just

mere roguery. 23. 16. There is a certain nobility about Sir
Toby. 13. When Sir Toby asks Malvolio, 'Dost thou think,
because thou art virtuous, there shall be no more cakes and
ale?' we rather tend to sympathize with him. 13. 5. 6. He
has a disliking for Malvolio's smugness and self-satisfac-
tion, and we dislike it too. 25. 16. We feel therefore, that we
have something in common with him, that we are both in
agreement over. 27. 16. Also, Sir Toby respects good
breeding, and he despises cowardice and treachery, and he
declares that Cesario is a 'very dishonest paltry boy' when
Sir Toby thinks that Cesario has betrayed Antonio. 7. 2.
13. He is no coward himself: he gets his sword out and is
ready to have a go if the occasion demands it. 23. 20. Also
he has enough conscience not to carry a joke too far and he
knows where to stop. 7. 16. He rebuked the Clown for
tormenting Malvolio, declaring that he does not want any
more such knavery: 'I would we were well rid of this
knavery.' 9. 30. Maybe the nicest thing about his character
was the fondness he had for Maria, showing that he has an
affectionate nature. 20. 18. 21. 9. 9. 12. Nevertheless we
perhaps feel a little sorry that Maria succeeds in becoming
Lady Belch because, we imagine, Sir Toby will be
persuaded by her to pack in his drinking, and we like him
best when he is half cut. 26. 20. 20.

Exercise 21

*This passage is full of tautological expressions, and of other kinds of
empty verbiage.*

It can be quite truthfully stated that Cassius is a man who is
all too capable of revealing the worst side to his character.
6. 15. Cassius seems to be a really unattractive person
during the earlier scenes of the play, being bitter and
irritable and edgy, and brooding over injustices. 13. 5. 2.

16. Mocking Caesar's physical weaknesses, and egging Brutus on, in a nasty sort of way, to join the conspiracy. 20. 20. 8. When he declares his intention of forging some letters to fool Brutus, we almost tend to expect that he is going to be the villain of the play. 20. 6. He is in the plot we feel, for personal gain, and Brutus definitely seems to be acting rightly and properly when he rebukes Cassius on this account. 27. 5. 16. 13.

It must be noted however, that as the play gets going some other things about Cassius's character come out. 6. 27. 20. 21. 20. We see that Cassius is in a way a more honest man than Antony, who does not hesitate to con friend and foe alike. 13. 6. 20. Also we see that his mind tends to be a good bit better than Brutus's. 7. 6. 20. 18. If he had had his way, instead of Brutus, the whole affair would have turned out a lot more successfully for the conspirators, and the plot would not have been a failure. 20. 20. 16. For example, he says that Antony should be murdered with Caesar, and he wants to refuse Antony permission to speak at the funeral and keep him silent, because Cassius is absolutely convinced that Antony's speech will start something up. 23. 16. 13. 5. 20. Finally, we see that he was a man of really warm feelings. 9. 5. The clearest example of the tenderness he is capable of is when he hears of Portia's death. 11. It would seem that he was sincerely and genuinely moved. 6. 9. 16. For a moment, when he hears from Brutus that she died by poison ('swallowed fire') he is so shocked and horrified that he is stuck for words. 30. 27. 16. 20. His tenderness is also shown in his attitude towards the rude and ill-mannered Casca, with whom he is gentle and mild and patient. 16. 16. These things in Cassius's character made him many friends and Titinius was one. 21. 2. Titinius thought such a lot of him that he had just no inclination or desire to live after Cassius's death. 20. 22. 16.

Exercise 22

Several colons and dashes are needed, if this passage is to be properly punctuated.

The snake, as Lawrence describes it, has two opposite aspects that are quite different from each other, it is mysteriously grand, and at the same time it is definitely ugly. 16. 28. 5. Lawrence just worships the grandeur and majesty of this creature. 22. 16. Throughout the poem he plugs the idea that it is like a king. 20. He talks about feeling honoured because it has left the underworld in order to get a drink at his trough, and he calls it 'one of the lords of life'. 20. 23. 23. In this way he puts over a real impression of its majesty, and of the sense of awe that he gets when he is in its presence. 20. 18. 23.

At the same time another influence is at work in Lawrence, the voice of his education. 28. This voice says to him that the snake is venomous and that he must kill the snake, rather than feel honoured at its presence. 23. 13. 15. But when it turns its back on him, and he threw a stick at it, he was suddenly filled with shame for having obeyed this voice ('the voices of accursed human education'). 9. 9. 30. He sums up his view of his behaviour in one word, 'vulgar'. 28.

The poem has a third feature to it, realistic description. 15. 28. It is absolutely full of good detail. 5. 18. The snake's 'yellow-brown slackness' is noticed by Lawrence, and he says how it 'softly drank through its straight gums'. 26. 23. Which creates such a clear picture. 8. 10. The realism of the description is further added to by some other details that Lawrence puts in. 24. 20. For example, he says how he is in his pyjamas because of the heat, and he names the tree, it has the strange-sounding name of 'carab', that stands nearby. 23. 28.

Thus the poem as a whole in a way consists of a marvellous blend of different points of view. 6. 18. Lawrence almost seems to become, during the course of it, three different people, an imaginative artist or poet, a civilized man of convention, and a good observer of nature. 28. 16. 18.

Exercise 23

Nearly all the quotations in this passage are wrongly introduced. The passage also lacks dignity; many of the words are drawn from slang expressions.

The whole course of the love of Romeo and Juliet, from beginning to end, is determined by the terrible feud between the Capulets and the Montagues. 16. 18. In the first moments of the play, before either Romeo or Juliet have come on, a quarrel starts up between the servants of the rival houses. 20. 20. The feud continues throughout the entire play, and it is only ended by the dreadful death of the lovers. 16. 18.

The fate of Romeo and Juliet is also determined by one bit of awful luck. 20. If Friar Laurence's message had reached Romeo, the final tragedy with which the play ends simply would not have occurred. 16. 22. The message did not reach him because of Friar John being delayed because the city authorities sealed up the doors of the house he was in. 25. 14.

The idea that the lovers are doomed is mentioned on numerous occasions during the course of the play. 19. The speaker of the Prologue calls them 'star-crossed'. 23. Also he says that 'nought could remove' the feud between the parents except 'but their children's end'. 7. 23. 32. Several mentions are made, during the course of the play, of fortune. 25. After Romeo has left, in the early morning,

Juliet says that fortune is fickle:

O fortune, fortune! all men call thee fickle. 23. 30.

Another example is when Friar Laurence, hearing that Friar John had not been able to get the letter to Romeo, says 'unhappy fortune!' 11. 9. 23. 23. In the last scene, after Romeo has killed Paris, Romeo calls himself a person whose name is written in 'sour misfortune's book'. 13. 23. The lovers themselves often express fears and anxieties about their future. 16. Before going to the Capulets' feast Romeo tells Benvolio of his fear of –

Some consequence yet hanging in the stars
Shall bitterly begin his fearful date
With this night's revels. 32.

Juliet had forebodings, too. 9. She is afraid, she tells Romeo, that their course of love –

It is too rash, too unadvis'd, too sudden. 32.

Later, in the scene at dawn, after Romeo has climbed down from the window, Juliet cried out that she had an 'ill-divining soul'. 9. 9. For one awful moment she imagines that she sees Romeo as a corpse in a tomb –

As one dead in the bottom of a tomb. 18. 30.

All of which makes one feel that no human power could have altered a thing. 8. 21.

Exercise 24

This is another passage in which many of the quotations are wrongly introduced.

The speeches that Romeo and Juliet say, as the day gets near, are absolutely full of descriptive poetry. 23. 23. 5.

Juliet tells Romeo how the nightingale –

Nightly she sings on yon pomegranate-tree –

and this naming of the tree adds a bit of realism to the scene. 32. 20. Romeo, in his reply, describes the dawn in a marvellous image, which he keeps up through several lines of poetry. 18. 20. He first says –

what envious streaks
Do lace the severing clouds in yonder east. 23. 32.

The word 'envious' puts across his own feelings on the dawn, he imagines that it envies the happiness which he and Juliet have shared together. 20. 15. 28. 16. The word 'lace' is a marvellous bit of description, for it builds up a good picture of the way in which the first streaks of daylight split the clouds. 18. 20. 20. 18. Romeo's next expression is even more imaginative still. 16. Romeo personifies the day, and says that the day is standing on tiptoe on the mountain-tops. 13. 23. 13. Juliet's reply, too, is ever so imaginative. 10. She says to him that the light is not the dawn, but a meteor of the sun:

It is some meteor that the sun exhales. 23. 30.

Romeo, in another flight of fancy, declares that he is ready to kid himself that the grey light –

'Tis but the pale reflex of Cynthia's brow. 20. 32.

Juliet then plays poetically with the word 'division', using this word both in its old sense, to mean 'music' and also in its ordinary sense. 15. 13. 27. Some people she remarks, say that the lark 'makes sweet division', but this idea is just not true, because this lark –

This doth not so, for she divideth us. 27. 22. 32.

These speeches, as well as being poetically good, are also

ever so true to the character of the lovers. 18. 10. Romeo is definitely scared when he first hears the lark, which is suggested by Juliet's use of the word 'fearful'. 5. 20. 12. He is so worried and anxious that at first he simply will not listen to her when she tries to say to him that it was the nightingale he heard. 16. 22. 23. Even though she pleads and begs him to believe her. 16. 8. But her words have so much loving persuasion in them that after a bit he gives in to her. 25. 20. If she wants him to stay he tells her, he is content to fool himself into thinking that –

I'll say yon grey is not the morning's eye. 27. 20. 32.

This remark really frightens Juliet, and her whole attitude completely changes. 5. 16. With a tone of sudden fear she says to Romeo that it is the lark, and she orders him to clear off quickly. 15. 23. 20. When he hears her words he becomes filled with gloom and despair. 16. He climbs down from the window, and as he is about to go off Juliet has a nasty feeling that he is going to die. 20. 20.

Exercises 25–36: A-level English Literature examination

Exercise 25

In his descriptions of the pilgrims Chaucer often puts in details of dress. 20. Some of the details are no more than mere passing touches, the purpose of which is to boost the realism of the description. 16. 20. For example, when Chaucer says that the Yeoman wore a green coat and hood his purpose is merely to brighten the picture with a bit of colour. 23. 20. Another example is when he says that the Ploughman wore a tabard, for this detail does no more than add a spot of realism to a portrait that would otherwise be too vague. 11. 23. 20. At other times however, details of dress are introduced by Chaucer for a different purpose, he includes them in order to put across the characters of the pilgrims. 27. 26. 28. 20. Three examples of this method of using detail are when he describes the Squire, the Nun, and the Wife of Bath. 11.

The Squire's clothes are just typical of the man. 22. His gown is so gaudy that Chaucer used a simile to convey its brightness, he compares the gown to a flowery meadow. 9. 28. 13. Also he mentions that it is short and that its sleeves were long and wide, and so we deduce that it is cut in the latest style. 7. 9. 19. These things bring over the gaiety of the Squire's disposition. 21. 20. A really fashionably dressed young man, simply full of life. 5. 22. 8.

The Nun's dress definitely suggests that she is rather vain and worldly. 5. 5. Chaucer describes her dress in such a way as to imply that she has deliberately got herself up as an attractive woman. 13. 20. She wore a neatly folded wimple, a very dainty cloak, and a marvellous golden brooch, showing that the Nun gives quite a bit of thought to her appearance. 9. 5. 18. 12. 13. 20.

The Wife of Bath's dress is described by Chaucer in great detail. 26. Chaucer describes her dress in such a way as to lead the reader to one firm conclusion about her, the Wife of Bath is a show-off. 13. 13. 28. 13. 20. Round her hips she wore a foot-mantle, and she makes absolutely sure that her legs are conspicuous by wearing bright red stockings and new shoes with spurs to them. 9. 5. 15. The Wife of Bath's clothes are like her character, bold and colourful. 13. 28.

Exercise 26

Prince Henry is Shakespeare's picture of a perfect ideal of a king. 16. Prince Henry is a skilled and expert warrior, whose soldierly appearance gets the admiration of everyone. 13. 16. 23. Vernon tells Hotspur how the Prince looked when he got on his horse. 23. Vernon describes how the Prince vaulted so easily into his seat that he looked –

As if an angel dropp'd down from the clouds. 13. 32.

Also the Prince is gentle, kind, and charitable. 7. 16. He was a man who (in the King's words) –

He hath a tear for pity. 9. 32.

But he is never weak, if he is 'incensed' he is 'flint'. 28.

In *Henry IV* two opposing ways of life are portrayed, the lofty and the mean, the noble and the base. 28. 16. There is never any doubt as to which of them the Prince will make choice of. 25. The Prince's association with low company is presented, throughout both parts of the play, as part of a deliberate and conscious policy to develop and extend his knowledge of human nature. 13. 16. 16. Warwick, for one, understands the set-up clearly: he realizes that the Prince 'but studies his companions' in the same way as he might study a foreign language ('a strange tongue') 20. 30. The Prince himself calls Falstaff and his companions 'base contagious clouds' which conceal the sun which he resembles. 23. 14. In the first scene of the second part of the play he is already commencing to prepare himself for the very heavy responsibilities which, after a short interval of time, he will have to shoulder. 19. 5. 19. He blames himself, towards the end of the scene, for messing about. 20. Later, in the tavern scene, he again rebukes himself for –

So idly to profane the precious time. 32.

Things like this prepare us for the final transformation of the Prince that takes place at the end of the play. 21. 16. The Prince's rejection of Falstaff is an act that we have been expecting from the beginning and so it does not surprise us. 13. 16. This act is an act of high and solemn dignity – an act that is worthy of the man whose reign, as Henry V, is now starting off. 13. 16. 20.

Exercise 27

With the Nun Chaucer's attitude is gently satirical. 15. He definitely smiles at some of her habits and at certain things in her character. 5. 21. Her table manners, for example, are described by Chaucer in detail, and he presents them in such a way as to reveal one fact very clearly, she had an exaggerated love of courtly refinement. 26. 13. 28. She never wet her fingers in her 'sauce deep', nor does she ever let food fall from her lips, and after every drink she always wiped her upper lip 'so clean' that there was just no grease at all left in the cup. 9. 16. 22. Chaucer sums all this up in one sentence, she set great store he tells us, on 'courtesy'. 12. 28. 27.

Some of Chaucer's remarks about the Nun have deliberate exaggeration, not enough to make Chaucer's attitude obvious, but enough to suggest that he is in a way smiling. 25. 28. 13. 6. One example is when he says how she would simply burst into tears if she saw a mouse 'caught in a trap'. 11. 23. 22. Also Chaucer has a quite open laugh at her on one occasion. 7. 13. 25. She spoke French he tells us, very well; then he adds, casually as though it did not matter much, that she spoke it according to the school of Stratford-at-Bow and that she knows absolutely nothing about the French that was spoken in Paris. 27. 27. 9. 5.

With the Friar Chaucer's attitude is entirely different. 15. We are left in no doubt about his feelings towards this man, he hates the Friar. 28. 13. For example, when describing the Friar's methods of obtaining money, he twice brings in the word 'pleasant' in a tone of real sarcasm. 20. 18. Also he describes the Friar's hypocritical arguments sarcastically, for he implies that these hypocritical arguments always led to the convenient conclusion that people should give money to the friars:

Men must give silver to the poor friars. 7. 13. 30.

It is significant that there is just not one bit of humour in the description of the Friar, showing that Chaucer thought that there was nothing to smile at in the character of this greedy, grasping, hypocritical man. 22. 20. 12. 16.

Exercise 28

In 'The Darkling Thrush' a scene of wintry desolation and barrenness is described by Hardy. 16. 26. To Hardy's mind the frost-bound, lifeless land seemed in a way like the corpse of the nineteenth century. 13. 9. 6. The sound of the wind reminds Hardy of a dirge, and the cloudy sky looks like the roof of a crypt, and it is the time, Hardy reflects, when the human spirit sinks really low. 13. 2. 13. 5. Suddenly a thrush commences singing. 19. But the poet does not take heart from the song, but he reflects that it perhaps means that somewhere there is a bit of hope, but, he decides, if there is any, it must dwell in some place of which he is not aware. 20. 14.

The poet brings in two marvellous similes. 20. 18. In the first one he says that the stems of the vines are like the 'strings of broken lyres'. 23. With this simile he not only puts over a good picture of the stems, but also, by using the word 'scores', he adds a bit of cruelty to the scene. 15. 20. 18. 20. The second simile is when he compares the outlines of the landscape to the dead corpse of the century. 11. 16. This image is in a way a rather more imaginative one, for it is based not so much on observation as on a real flight of fancy. 6. 5. 5. Another example of Hardy's descriptive power is when he uses the word 'dregs', for by means of this one syllable he puts across a sense of the profound desolation of winter. 11. 20. Also his description of the thrush is good. 7. 18. He pictures a real bird – 'frail, gaunt and small' – and not a romantic creature, such as might have been thought up by some less truthful or honest poet. 20. 16.

The poem has a very regular metre to it, and the rhymes are very clear and musical. 5. 15. 5. Also there is some alliteration. 7. The rhymes and the alliteration combine together to form a beauty of sound; and this beauty serves to deepen the sadness. 16. 6. For one part of Hardy's theme was that the century had just died and that the wind is moaning in a 'death-lament'. 9. 9. By using words with open vowel-sounds Hardy makes the poem itself sound like a lament, his words really echo the cry of the wind. 13. 28. 5.

It is worth pointing out that the poem is thoroughly honest. 6. Hardy does not fool himself: on the contrary, he openly and frankly says that he cannot share the hope which the bird seems to feel. 20. 16. 23. In this respect he is rather superior to some other poets, who might have tried to convince themselves that they got inspiration from the bird's song. 5. 23.

Exercise 29

The poem that the Reverend Eli Jenkins recites has simplicity and sincerity, being a direct and straightforward tribute to the beauty of Llaregyb, where he has spent his life. 25. 2. 16. This small village is compared by him, in modest and humble terms, to a number of places in Wales famous for their beauty, and he decides that he simply would not exchange the village for any of these places. 26. 16. 22. 13. 13. There is a deep emotion to his words. 15. When Dylan Thomas wrote these lines he deliberately and consciously set out to write a poem of sentimentality, in other words, to write the sort of poem that we would expect the Reverend Eli Jenkins to say. 16. 25. 28. 23.

On the whole the technique of the poem, like the subject-matter, is simple, being written in ballad-measure and having clear, musical rhymes. 6. 2. Dylan Thomas relieves the monotony of the metre in two ways, he puts in several feminine rhymes, and he continues and extends some of his sentences across the divisions between the verses. 28. 20. 16. The feminine rhymes add to the musical beauty of the poem, and the long sentences somehow seem to allow the great emotion behind the words time to develop and die off again. 24. 6. 6. 18. 15. The beauty of sound is further added to by the rather lengthy list of nice-sounding Welsh names. 24. 5. 19. 18. Indeed, the climax to the poem is when the Reverend Eli Jenkins, after saying through the names of many rivers, suddenly turns his thoughts back to his own river Dewi. 15. 11. 23. The contrast he achieves is striking, for the Dewi is both very tiny in comparison with these other grand rivers, and also, unlike these rivers, the Dewi is simple and humble and unpretentious in the very sound of its name. 5. 13. 13. 16. The imagery used in the poem has both simplicity and aptness. 25. 25. For example, when the Reverend Eli Jenkins calls the Dewi 'a baby on a rushy bed' he is using words which are simple but which at the same time have associations which connect them with the Bible. 23. 14. Things like this link the poem with the character of the Reverend Eli Jenkins. 21. 13. They make us feel that the narrator's description of the poem is indeed a very true one, it is a 'morning service'. 5. 28.

Exercise 30

Nearly all the quotations in this passage are wrongly introduced.

We hear music on a considerable number of occasions on Prospero's island, and an important part is played by it in creating an atmosphere of supernatural strangeness. 19. 26. The first example of it is when we see Ferdinand following Ariel's 'sweet air'. 11. The music, which keeps starting up and then stopping absolutely astonishes him. 20. 5. He says how the music crept past him along the water, when he was sitting on a bank, and –

. . . thence have I followed it. 23. 13. 32.

The song carries on, and after a while he begins to be able to figure out some of its words. 20. 20. It reminds him, he declares –

The ditty does remember my drown'd father. 32.

We again hear music in the scene with Alonso and his followers. 15. Ariel wants to get some of them off to sleep and so 'solemn music' is played by him. 23. 26. A little later he comes on again and sings in Gonzalo's ear in order to get him up from sleep before Antonio and Sebastian murder him. 20. 23. The song was heard quite plainly by Gonzalo, for he remarks to Alonso afterwards that 'I heard a humming'. 9. 26. 32.

Also Ariel uses music to lead Caliban and Stephano and Trinculo out of their way. 7. He starts it up when they are singing a very drunken song of their own, and when Stephano and Trinculo hear it they are simply terrified. 20. 5. 22. Caliban tells them not to be afraid ('be not afeard'), and in a marvellous passage of poetry he goes on to explain that the island is haunted by music:

Sounds and sweet airs that give delight and hurt not. 30. 18. 32.

Then Trinculo notices that –

The sound is going away; let's follow it, and after do our work. 32.

Stephano agrees to follow; but he seems a bit reluctant, for he declares that he wishes 'I could see this taborer'. 20. 32.

Music is heard on numerous further occasions during the run of the play. 19. 20. Music is heard when the 'Shapes' come on; Iris and Ceres say their speeches to its accompaniment; and a bit more comes in when the nymphs and reapers dance. 13. 20. 23. 20. 20. Finally it is twice heard in the last scene, once when Alonso and the others walk into the charmed circle that Prospero has prepared, and again when the very last song in the play is sung by Ariel. 28. 5. 26. Apparently this song seems to move Prospero, for when it is over he tells Ariel sadly that 'I will miss thee'. 16. 32.

Exercise 31

This is another passage in which the quotations are wrongly introduced.

Several touches of character are given by Shakespeare to the ghost of Hamlet's father. 26. It is not an aggressive or pushing ghost, but on the contrary an almost timid ghost. 16. 13. When Horatio orders it to 'I charge thee speak!' it hurries off ('stalks away') as though offended. 32. 30. Later, at its second appearance, as soon as it hears the cock crow it 'started like a guilty thing' and vanishes. 32. Horatio gives a description of its expression to Hamlet, it showed, Horatio tells Hamlet,

A countenance more in sorrow than in anger. 25. 28. 13. 13.

When the ghost meets Hamlet it (as Horatio exclaims in amazement) 'beckons you to go with it'. 32. Marcellus watches it beckoning, and he notes its courteous gestures ('with what courteous action'). 30. Its very first words are to tell Hamlet that 'my hour is almost come' when it must give itself up again to 'tormenting flames'. 5. 32. Its tone is sad and mournful, so mournful that Hamlet says 'alas, poor ghost!' 16. 28. 23. The tale it imparts to Hamlet is so pitiful. 19. 10. On numerous occasions, during the course of its long speech, it sighs, and once it pauses in alarm ('methinks I scent the morning air'). 19. 32. The climax is when it describes, with a horrified tone, how Hamlet's uncle committed the murder:

And in the porches of my ears did pour
The leperous distilment. 11. 15. 32.

The effect was simply horrible. 22. The poison –

Swift as quicksilver it courses through

120

The natural gates and alleys of the body

- and within seconds it had covered the King's skin with rough sores ('with vile and loathsome crust'). 32. 30.

After it has concluded its narrative the ghost shows a touch of unexpected kindness, it begs Hamlet not to –

nor let thy soul contrive
Against thy mother aught. 19. 19. 28. 32.

On one more occasion, later in the play, when Hamlet is with his mother, the same kindliness of character is exhibited by it. 26. 19. It is saddened and grieved to see the look of amazement on her face, and it begs Hamlet to –

O, step between her and her fighting soul. 16. 32.

Exercise 32

Several colons and dashes are needed, if this passage is to be properly punctuated.

Falstaff's most obvious and noticeable characteristic can be easily defined, he is a buffoon. 16. 28. His other characteristics, his moodiness, his selfishness, his vanity, are not so apparent. 28. That is why we so readily notice, as something inescapably obvious and plain to see, the change that comes over Falstaff in the second part of *Henry IV*. 16. 13. In this play his buffoonery is toned down sharply, so sharply, in fact, that his other characteristics definitely begin to come to the fore. 28. 5. Shakespeare had a reason for this, he wanted to get the audience ready for the Prince's rejection of Falstaff at the end of the play. 12. 28. 23.

When we first see Falstaff in this play he is disgruntled and sullen and very sulky. 16. 5. He has perhaps some excuse, his Page is making him look daft. 28. 20. But at the end of the scene, when he is left on his own, Falstaff goes in for a bit of grumbling and grousing for its own sake. 13. 20. 20. 16. In the street scene, the scene in which he appears with Fang and Snare, we notice a change, his moodiness seems to have gone off and he is without doubt more like his old self. 28. 28. 20. 6. But in the tavern scene Falstaff gets moody again. 13. 23. The things he says about the Prince and Poins are genuinely bitter, and from time to time he gets morbid and begins to harp on the fact that he is growing old. 21. 23. 20. A little later, in the scene in which he comes on with Justice Shallow, he is more solemn and serious than we would have expected. 20. 16. He is somehow withdrawn, and not at all anxious to listen to Shallow's reminiscences about the past. 6. 16. We can guess the reason, these reminiscences remind him of his age. 28. 13. In the second part, too, one other aspect of Falstaff's character comes up more and more clearly, his coarseness. 20. 28. In the first part Falstaff is nothing more than just a buffoon. 13. 16. In the second part he rather degenerates, in fact he becomes a debauched old rascal. 5. 28.

The rejection of Falstaff in the last scene of the play is really moving. 18. At this last moment Falstaff is such a sad figure. 13. 10. The sadness, and Shakespeare often uses this technique, is added to by means of contrast, for we have just witnessed an outburst of delight from Falstaff, which he gave way to in Shallow's house when he got the news of the King's death. 28. 24. 23. At the very end, when the blow falls, everything that is most genuine and real in him comes up. 16. 20. He stands still for a moment in absolutely baffled silence, he has one last go at reasserting the old self-confidence, he makes one last appeal, and then finally, and it is the one truly noble act of his life, he faces the truth and walks away with bravery. 5. 20. 28. 25.

Exercise 33

Several colons and dashes are needed, if this passage is to be properly punctuated.

The opening lines of 'Anthem for Doomed Youth' are so bitter. 10. The men who died in battle the poet implies, were doubly insulted, they were deprived of a funeral service, and at the same time they were given a grim and horrible parody of a funeral service. 27. 28. 16. 13. The only salute they got was 'the monstrous anger of the guns', and the only prayer that was said for these men was just the mutter of rifle fire. 23. 13. 16. The poet puts across his bitterness by bringing in the word 'choirs' in a double sense, at their funeral service, the poet writes, these men did have choirs, the choirs of wailing shells. 20. 20. 28. 13. 28.

The sestet has a different tone, there being a prevalence of a mood of gentleness and pity. 28. 25. It is as though the poet, after getting his bitterness out, must now express his deep sorrow and grief. 23. 16. In this part of the poem the poet manages to look on the dead soldiers from the point of view of the dead soldiers' relatives and sweethearts. 13. 6. 13. The grief that these people felt, he implies, is the real funeral tribute that the young men get. 9. 23. These closing lines are emotional and deeply felt. 16. The words have gentleness and sadness, and the poet's profound sense of pity is expressed by them. 25. 25. 26.

The imagery has both simplicity and vividness. 25. 25. The simile, 'die as cattle', puts over perfectly the point that the poet wishes to impress on the reader, that the lives of the young men are held cheap. 20. 28. The second image, 'the monstrous anger of the guns', suggests two things, it suggests that war is brutal and bestial, and also that is it monstrously wrong. 21. 28. 16. In the expression, 'the shrill demented choirs of wailing shells', the lenghty vowel-sounds of the words 'choirs' and 'wailing' tend to increase the effect. 19. 6. 24. In the sestet the poet relies more on beauty of diction rather than on imagery or figurative expressions. 16. 16. 'Holy', 'flowers', 'tenderness', 'dusk', these words put a note of sadness and beauty into the closing lines. 28. 20.

Exercise 34

The style of this passage is heavy; the writer has a habit of choosing pompous words and expressions.

Keats begins by examining the urn, and he revolves it this way and that so as to see its different sides and facets, and he wonders what stories its pictures communicate. 2. 19. 16. 19. Then Keat's imagination assumes control, and the pictures begin to come to life. 13. 19. There are two figures in the first scene he looks at, a youth and a maiden. 28. The youth is about to bestow a kiss on his loved one, but he will never be able to do so, says Keats, on account of the fact that he is only a figure in a picture and is therefore incapable of motion. 19. 23. 19. 19. But he has a consolation, his loved one, being also part of the picture too, must remain forever 'fair'. 28. 16.

The poem attains to a climax in the third verse. 19. The urn is now completely and entirely forgotten by Keats and he steps into the world that its pictures delineate. 16. 26. 19. It is an idealized world of perfection, in which the trees can never 'shed your leaves', and in which the melodies that the youth is piping continue forever ('For ever piping songs for ever new'). 16. 32. 32. Then the vase is again turned by Keats, so that different pictures come into view, and he engages in a contemplation of two more scenes. 26. 25. First the scene of the sacrifice, and then after that the little town. 8. 16. They receive a less rapturous description than the earlier scene, but they are more closely and sharply detailed. 25. 16. We are presented with a glimpse of a 'green altar', a heifer dressed for sacrifice ('with garlands drest'), and a 'mountain-built' town. 19. 30.

In the last verse Keats returns, and the word 'O' suggests that he does so with a sigh, to the world of reality. 28. Once again the urn is consciously contemplated by him, and he marvels at the way in which it had set his imagination functioning. 26. 19. But the flight of fancy from which he has returned has brought about a strengthening and deepening of his belief in the power of beauty. 25. 16. Now he too, like the youth in the picture, can attain to some consolation, it lies in the fact that the urn itself, which is an object of beauty, will endure and last on through the ages. 19. 28. 16.

Exercise 35

This passage contains some unnecessarily pompous words, and some of the sentences are not as clear as they should be because the writer has used abstract nouns instead of expressing himself concretely and directly.

A major proportion of the cause of Othello's tragedy can be traced to his colour. 19. 25. There must have been a prevalence, we feel, among the Venetians of that day, of strong racial prejudices. 25. For example, although Brabantio holds admiration for Othello, and on numerous occasions invites him to his house, he is horrified by the prospect of having Othello as a son-in-law. 25. 19. 13. Iago, too, revealed his prejudice when he threw mud at Othello's blackness in the first scene. 9. 9. 20. Another example is towards the end of the play when Emilia cries out to

Othello about Desdemona that –

She was too fond of her most filthy bargain. 11. 32.

These things must have made a big impression on Othello.
21. 18. One of his first thoughts, when he begins to hold
suspicions in relation to Desdemona, is that her unfaithful-
ness towards him has arisen from the fact that he is black.
25. 25. Because he has this deep sensitivity in him, Iago's
poisonous suggestions are more readily accepted by him.
25. 26. He is so deeply hurt that he just cannot bear to bring
his torment into the open by instituting an investigation.
22. 19.

Also Othello's colour is the cause of his tragedy in a very
much deeper sense, for it has moulded Othello's whole
character. 7. 5. 13. Every phase of his behaviour reveals a
nature that has both more strength and more simplicity in
it than that of a white person. 25. 25. He maintains calm-
ness superbly, for example, when Brabantio and his
followers challenge him. 25. Again, when he silenced the
brawl that starts up during Cassio's watch, he exhibits the
same mastery over himself. 9. 20. 19. But his self-control,
we feel, is too strong, too inflexible, too rigid, for when he
does undergo a loss of this self-control he undergoes a
complete loss of it. 16. 25. 13. 25. There are absolutely no
half-measures with him. 5. A remark that illustrates this
aspect of his character very clearly is when he tells Iago
that he could follow no middle course, it had to be either
complete love or complete jealousy. 11. 28. In fact, it could
be stated that he is like a child. 6. As such, he is so easily
ensnared by Iago's dreadful intrigues. 10. 18.

Thus Othello's character, which is related to his colour,
worked against him in two ways, it results in his trusting a
wicked villain, and in his being liable to act with
impulsiveness and violence. 9. 28. 16. 25. 25.

Exercise 36

The style of this passage is laboured. The writer has a way of needlessly twisting his statements into the passive, of introducing abstract nouns unnecessarily, and of choosing stilted expressions.

In the first scene with Ophelia both her brother and her father give her advice not to place trust in Hamlet's professions of love. 15. 25. 25. She does not openly and directly contradict what they say, but her manner carries the implication that she does not agree with them and that she holds a firm belief in Hamlet's sincerity. 16. 25. 25. When Laertes states that Hamlet's admiration for her is no more than a passing fancy, she replies 'No more but so' in a tone of doubting disbelief. 19. 16. Again, when her brother has concluded his lengthy sermon on the dangers of being too forward, Ophelia answers her brother in a spirit of good-humoured irony. 19. 19. 13. 13. She is equally firm when her father endeavours to convince her that Hamlet is trifling. 19. She does not answer her father directly when he questions her, and when he scoffs at her and chides her she continues in the maintenance of her point of view. 13. 16. 25. Hamlet, she insists, pledged his love for her with a solemn vow, which annoys her father so much that he at once goes on to make an angry speech in which he issues a veto against her having any future meetings with Hamlet. 12. 25.

Before a great deal of time has elapsed Ophelia is to be cruelly disillusioned. 19. Blow after blow is suffered by her. 26. First (as she recounts to her father afterwards) Hamlet simply terrifies her by bursting in upon her while she is sewing in her room. 19. 22. Next she is constrained to converse with him while her father and the King listen. 19. 19. Finally, on top of all these things, the sudden shock of her father's death has to be suffered by her. 21. 16. 26.

127

Ophelia's sufferings undermine her sanity and in the last scene in which she appears she dashes into the Queen's presence and gazes at her without recognizing her. 2. 20. She is carrying a lute, and she commences singing. 19. After two or three verses have been sung by her the King comes on, but she is so distracted that she does not notice him and she continues with her song unheeding and all who are watching her pity her very much. 26. 20. 2. 18. Even the King. 8. Then she goes out into the garden and returns, after a comparatively short interval of time, carrying flowers and herbs, her purpose being, it seems, to use these flowers and herbs as part of her father's funeral service, which she now imagines is taking place, for she hands them to the people near her, apparently labouring under the misconception that she is giving them to her fellow-mourners. 19. 2. 13. 19. Her last words are a prayer, in a devout and reverent whisper she asks God to have mercy. 28. 16.